In Search of Music Education

In Search of *Music Education*

Estelle R. Jorgensen

University of Illinois Press

Urbana and Chicago

Library of Congress Cataloging-in-Publication Data
Jorgensen, Estelle Ruth.
    In search of music education / Estelle R. Jorgensen.
      p.   cm.
    Includes bibliographical references and index.
    ISBN 0-252-06609-X (pbk : acid-free paper).
    ISBN 0-252-02307-2 (cloth : acid-free paper)
    1. Music—Instruction and study. I. Title.
MT1.J676   1997   96–25326
780′.7—dc20   CIP
                                 MN

For Faye

Contents

Preface

Every book has a story, and this one is no exception. The questions with which it grapples have preoccupied me for more than two decades. I have been puzzled about how people come to know music, how so many diverse musical traditions and ways of teaching and learning music have emerged throughout the world, how musical and social systems maintain themselves, and what the responsibilities of musicians, teachers, and the public are to this multiplicity of musical and educational beliefs and practices. Over the years, these questions become more insistent, more important, and more problematical. It was tempting to wait until a fuller, richer, truer vision emerged rather than plunge into a book that could only promise incomplete answers. A conviction settled, however, that there are at least some things that can and should be said about music education at this time. And I shall undertake to address them here in the hope of examining the others another day.

Since music entered public education in the nineteenth century, music education has often been thought of narrowly and unsatisfactorily in terms of incomplete musical tasks and objectives, elementary and intermediate levels of musical instruction carried out in the context of state-supported schools, and identified especially with music of the Western classical tradition. Sometimes regarded as the poor sister of music performance, history, theory, and composition or uneasily situated under the umbrella of general education, music education has come to be regarded as a field of study that concerns itself only with music instruction in elementary and secondary schools.

This focus has gone largely unchallenged for two reasons. First, in the West, elementary and secondary schooling typically comprise the compulsory general education of citizens, and the attention of music educators has naturally gravitated there. In the United States, as in other countries, interest has centered particularly on the needs and interests of teachers of bands, choirs, and general music in elementary and secondary schools. If music constitutes a part of compulsory, state-mandated education, many believe, its objectives and methods should be at the heart of music education. Teachers should be equipped to offer musical instruction in these elementary and secondary schools, and music educators in the academy should be preoccupied with preparing them for these instructional situations.

Second, music educators typically value solutions to their questions more than the questions themselves. They are often more interested in positing practical answers to the issues they face than in raising questions about the underlying assumptions and methods they have espoused. Many have not learned to love the questions themselves; they have been uncomfortable with the ambiguities, discontinuities, and dialectics encountered in the practice of music education. Consequently, ideas lacking immediate practical application to the worlds of elementary and secondary school music teaching are sometimes dismissed as of little consequence, and researchers feel it incumbent on themselves to make immediate practical applications of their findings, even if these are somewhat premature. This quest for definitive solutions can readily be explained as follows. The people who are attracted to music education are often practical-minded and less interested in theorizing than in doing. Teachers who are trained as technicians to follow prescribed instructional methods often feel ill-equipped to grapple with the difficult philosophical and practical challenges they face, many of which require immediate solution. And the field of music education construed as school music represents a comparatively young scholarly tradition still in the process of clearly defining and defending itself.

The preoccupation of music educators with elementary and secondary school music, and their quest for immediate practical solutions, are problematical ideas. Regarding the first, the preoccupation of music educators with elementary and secondary school music, it should be remembered that for the greater part of history a different view of music education prevailed. Music education was conducted in families, churches, private music studios, universities, conservatories, and businesses, among other places. It included music instruction from elementary to advanced levels of musical proficiency. And it was and still is conducted around the world in ways that differ significantly from the comparatively limited array of instructional methods followed by school musicians in the West. If we take a global rather than ethnocentric view of music education, it will be important to broaden our view to include a plethora of instances and approaches besides school music that may also count as music education.

Regarding the second, the quest for practical solutions, not only are the questions music educators face particularly perplexing and intractable but also, in spite of some bright prospects, a sense that all is not well in the world of music and music education pervades some quarters of the profession. The reasons for this malaise are readily apparent. Recently in the West, public demand for educational accountability has implied a lack of public confidence in what school music teachers are doing and have done in the past. Many state-run schools lack the financial resources to mount and sustain quality music programs. Under this pressure, at least in the United States, music supervisors, consultants, and other music educators, whose job it once was to forge a rapprochement between the world of music and that of general education, have begun to disappear. Population migrations around the world, coupled with the pervasive influence of Western popular musics, have also prompted music teachers to wonder what they should teach to a diverse population of students who are enamored of popular musics and seemingly indifferent to others. Many voices speak of the intrinsic importance of music in general education and its humanizing qualities— its contribution to spiritual, imaginative, and social life. Yet these voices sometimes seem lost in the chorus of those demanding of the schools' accountability, economic and technological supremacy, and cognitive skills of the sort required for computation, reading comprehension, factual recall, and the like. Increasingly, the old answers to questions regarding theoretical and practical questions in music education no longer suffice, and new paradigms need to be forged. Music educators are faced with radically rethinking their objectives and methods, a prospect that naturally meets with resistance from those who are comfortable with the way things are.

How a profession conceives of itself, its reason for being, and its assumptions about the world with which it interacts has much to do with how it goes about doing what it does and practicing what it professes. The assumptions underlying music education largely shape its particular objectives and methods. If it is thought of narrowly as elementary and secondary school music, a different range of objectives and methods will be evident than if it is thought of broadly in the way I suggest in these pages. Rethinking music education is a difficult task, conceptually and practically. Conceiving of alternative ideas and strategies is not easy, and getting them accepted or put into practice is challenging. Yet music educators and those interested in their work should not be deterred from tackling the problems of how music education can and should be undertaken.

I do not offer a definitive practical plan for music education. Rather, I wish to suggest significant theoretical questions and principles that may constitute a basis upon which such a plan may eventually be built and that ultimately have significant implications for the practice of music education. Actions flow from underlying assumptions, and examining assumptions provides important clues to the nature of practices that flow from them. Questions provide a means of getting at these underlying assumptions and a starting point for any analysis of the practice of music education. Dealing with these questions requires systematic reflection about theoretical issues and their implications for practice. Only then are music education policy-makers in a position to tackle the different and problematical task of translating these ideas into practice.

My central question in the following chapters concerns the nature of music education. In attempting to redefine its scope and nature I argue for a broadly based view that has global implications and a long, distinguished history stretching back to antiquity. Examples of music education turn up in unexpected places, including the efforts of family members, professional musicians, conservatory, college, and university professors, church musicians, business people, and a host of others engaged in the process of passing on musical wisdom from one generation to the next. Music education involves life-long teaching and learning, from the most elementary through the most advanced levels of musical artistry within the purview of a variety of societal institutions and exemplifying the gamut of world musical traditions. As an interdisciplinary field, music education draws from diverse literatures, including anthropology, sociology, psychology, religion, philosophy, ethnomusicology, music, and education.

In proposing such a broad concept of music education, I am also committed to the idea that music educators need to embrace the many discontinuities, dissonances, and dialectics of their world. The multiplicities and pluralities of individuals bring us face to face with the challenges of reconciling differences in language, culture, religion, life-style, age, and color, among a host of other boundaries that separate people. Notwithstanding technological advances that have made knowledge of formerly remote events more accessible than in the past, misunderstandings, tensions, and hostilities still abound.

The best way to meet these challenges is to take a dialectical and dialogical view of music education, recognize tensions in need of resolution, and hope that through dialogue these tensions can be worked through and either reconciled or tolerated. Such a view implies that there is no one high road to music education, no one instructional method that fits all, and no one technology appropriate for every situation. Teachers need to assume the role of professionals rather than technicians, analyze their particular situations, and provide what in their judgment will be the most effective sorts of instruction. They need to reflect on their circumstances critically and construct appropriate strategies accordingly.

In drawing the threads of music education so broadly, I revisit key concepts respecting the nature of music and education. The task of further extending this analysis, fleshing out many of its aspects, and deducing its practical applications to music education is inviting. In the process, many other views of music and education will intersect. My approach to music education finds its home within the philosophical tradition of John Dewey, Paulo Freire, Maxine Greene, Susanne Langer, Israel Scheffler, and Alfred North Whitehead, among others. Within music education, many connections with the ideas of such writers as John Blacking, Patricia Shehan Campbell, David Elliott, Lucy Green, Vernon Howard, Anthony Kemp, James Mursell, Anthony Palmer, Bennett Reimer, Abraham Schwadron, John Shepherd, Christopher Small, and Keith Swanwick will become clear along the way.

What follows constitutes a three-part analysis, each focusing on a particular question. Although each chapter stands independently, they might usefully be read in order. In the first, "In Search of Music Education," I ask what is meant by the word *education*. Opting to look first at the nature of education, I examine and criticize an illustrative list of five very different concepts of education in music: schooling, training, eduction, socialization, and enculturation. Each of these terms invokes a different concept of what education should be and is. Each has advantages and disadvantages, which I illustrate with various examples. Criticizing these views may suggest alternative solutions, some of which may be similar, whereas others may be ambiguous, even contradictory. Each concept provides a unique perspective on the educational process yet is lacking in one respect or another and requires reconciliation. In espousing a dialectical view such as this, I am left with education's inherent ambiguity and problematical character and a nest of difficult questions; for example, How can music educators reconcile these more-or-less conflicting concepts of education?

In "On Spheres of Musical Validity" I tackle the question of what is meant by the word *music*. This is a tantalizing and difficult problem. I narrow the search and discover how it is that groups of people come to share certain understandings and expectations about musical belief and practice and how they are able to maintain certain corporate identities as groups or institutions. Five processes—focusing, in turn, on the family, religion, politics, the music profession, and commerce—demonstrate how musical groups form and maintain themselves. Each process is explained and illustrated by means of a wide array of examples drawn from various literatures, and each is in tension with the others. Understanding music in this way, as social as well as individual experience, provides compelling reasons why music education should be construed to encompass an array of societal institutions and why its conception as public or state-supported music education cannot suffice. A complex array of questions further compounds the problem of music education, one of which concerns how music educators are to reconcile these sometimes conflicting social and musical processes.

Adding fuel to the fire but at the same time effecting a synthesis of sorts, "A Dialectical View of Music Education" traces some of the tensions that such a broad view of music education raises, particularly those related to musical form and context, great and little musical traditions, transmission and transformation, continuity and interaction, making and receiving, understanding and pleasure, philosophy and practice, and implications for music education practice. The chapter is a consideration of how music educators are to reconcile the dialectics that combining music and education, each with its own particular complexities, initiates. These dialectics suggest an enormously problematical and daunting vision of music education. Nevertheless, they reflect the inherent nature of the music education enterprise and the complexity of the world in which it takes place. Paradoxically, through complicating the task of music education and grappling with these challenges, music education's reason for being can be better grounded and its future secured.

How to design a practical system of music education that fosters such a dialectical vision? In resisting the temptation to spell out a practical solution to the problems raised, I return to my assumption that the search for principles undergirding music education is of the greatest importance, even more immediate than devising practical solutions. Theoretical principles have within them the seeds of practical strategies. They imply solutions yet to come. They are also ambiguous. Each principle may suggest various practical solutions more or less consistent with it. Even those dialectical tensions that may turn out to be practically insoluble and must therefore be lived with rather than brought into harmony are anchoring points. They suggest underlying principles of reciprocity, equity, inclusiveness, mutual respect, restraint, balance, democracy, and dialogue rooted in the ethical obligations of music educators.

The vision of music education offered in these pages is suggestive rather than prescriptive, necessitating the teacher's reason, intuition, imagination, and feeling to flesh it out. That is both the strength and the limitation of my contribution. I offer general principles of music education that may be helpful in analyzing its scope and nature. Music educators are entrusted with creating solutions appropriate to their particular circumstances in their individual ways. By framing and birthing their own solutions, they are empowered as artists to seek the most effective strategies for their learning communities.

Acknowledgments

I am deeply indebted to my students, colleagues, and friends at Indiana University School of Music, particularly the community of fellow travelers who love the questions and have conversed with me on various themes I take up in these pages. I especially appreciate the critical eyes and helpful comments of Austin Caswell, George Heller, and Iris Yob, who read the entire manuscript, and Charles Schmidt, who read parts of it. The company I keep, however, should not be blamed for my particular foibles. I take full responsibility for my ideas. Thanks are also due to Karen Gast for preparing the manuscript and Judith McCulloh and Mary Giles of the University of Illinois Press for their editorial guidance.

In Search of Music Education

Music making is a characteristically human activity. It is so pervasive that it appears to be universal. From antiquity, people have been making music, whether singing, playing instruments, or dancing, in religious rituals, family festivals, theatrical spectacles, political events, musical concerts, and a host of other social occasions. An enormous variety of musical expressions and a plethora of musical beliefs, customs, and traditions exist throughout the world. As a social activity, music making brings together composers, performers, and listeners in an experience that is meaningful and significant, collectively shared and personally understood. Music seems to transcend cultural boundaries because its significance may be grasped, at least partly, by others from different social and cultural backgrounds, yet it is also intimately bound to a particular social group or society, and outsiders cannot fully understand it.

Seeing that music making is so widespread in so many forms, it is not surprising to find correspondingly diverse varieties of musical education. Without music education, it would be impossible for each social group or society to sustain itself and replenish its supply of composers, performers, and listeners who understand the significance of musical events and can participate meaningfully in the occasions of music making.[1] Throughout history, there have been numerous instances of music education under the auspices of states, families or clans, music professionals, churches, and commercial businesses. It has been influenced by inventors who have brought about technological changes in music and music making, patrons who have sponsored musicians and organized musical events, and population migrations (both forced and voluntary) that have brought together people whose musics differ. And it has varied in the complexity of the musical materials to be mastered; the age, gender, ethnic background, and social status of the participants; and their instructional objectives and methods, among a host of other characteristics.

This variety of examples of music education causes us to wonder how it might be defined globally to transcend its traditional equation in the West with music in elementary and secondary schools. If evidence shows that music education has occurred in many places besides schools, and at other times, a broader view of the field is called for that opens possibilities for the contributions of other agencies to be counted as music education. My goal is to begin to flesh out what such a broad view of music education might look like and ask, What is music education?

At least two contrasting stances might be adopted in seeking to understand music education. First, assuming that Western classical music represents the epitome of musical development and Western music education is the ideal or quintessential form of music education, only Western music and music education are worthy of study. Other forms of musical education, especially those in preliterate or preindustrial societies, cannot safely be relied upon to provide a sound basis for musical instruction. Second, our study broadens to include all forms of music education, irrespective of their societal derivation. When world musics are assumed to be understood contextually and comparatively according to many different value systems, Western classical music is seen as only one of many diverse musics rather than the ideal, each music is properly studied within the context of its own tradition in ways consistent with that particular musical tradition, and Western musical education is only one of many ways by which people come to know music.

The latter view offers a contextual rather than an idealistic view of music making and music education, a basis for a broad and dispassionate view of music education, one that seeks to be faithful to all the classical, folk, and popular musical traditions of the world (in comparison to the more limited and culturally biased conception of music education implied in the former view).[2] In a particular set of practical circumstances, a teacher may choose to adopt a more limited perspective of his or her task that reflects elements of the first view. In the broader context of a theoretical description of music education as a historical and global phenomenon, however, the latter view may offer more scope and promise than the former.

Moreover, this stance seems relevant to, and serves a useful purpose within, an alternative paradigm that has been emerging, particularly since the 1960s.[3] Among the various statements of this worldview, the Gaia hypothesis posits that all things on planet earth comprise part of an interconnected dynamic system in delicate balance, where the whole transcends the sum of its parts.[4] Applied figuratively in the social realm, this hypothesis challenges the rule of technology, positivism, and rationality and posits the complementarity of the arts, the validity of nonscientific ways of knowing, and the importance of imagination and intuition. Its concern is with process as well as product, with cooperation along with competition, and it suggests that feminine in addition to masculine ways of knowing enhance the richness of human society and personal well-being. In the present climate of economic, political, and cultural internationalism, it implies that music should be studied as a world rather than just as a Western phenomenon, holistically and contextually rather than atomistically and separate from the rest of human experience.

A global view of music education such as that just described is compatible with, and would help foster, the kind of international cooperation that the Gaia hypothesis implies. A comparative and contextual study of world musics can help students understand cultures other than their own and intuitively and imaginatively grasp the perspectives and expressions of others—what people have in common and how they differ—and foster tolerance of cultural differences with people in other societies, thereby providing a better basis for cooperation.[5]

Assuming that music education is to be found in societies throughout the world under the aegis of various social institutions impacted by social developments of various kinds and exemplifying many instructional methods and demographic characteristics, what, taking a contextual, inclusive, and egalitarian approach to world musics and music education, is the essence of the discipline? What makes these disparate instances music education? What characteristics do they share? In what respects do they differ? Is there a systematic way of describing this variety of what may be thought of as instances of music education?[6]

This puzzle has two parts, each having to do with the conception of music education. The first part concerns the nature of education; the second, the nature of music. Both aspects are essential to a fuller understanding of what is encompassed within music education. I shall tackle this issue by assuming, for the present, a socially based definition of what music is, leaving it to those within a given society to describe what they understand to be music. This assumption is problematical; people sometimes disagree about the status of a particular music and its validity and place within the accepted corpus of musical instances accepted as music. There is general consensus about what counts as music in a particular society, however, and I will present the case for this assumption in chapter 2. Here, my focus is on what is meant by education and discovering how people come to know music (assuming that there is general agreement on what it is). I shall explore several conceptions of music education that have been evident historically, words that have been employed to describe education: *schooling, training, education, socialization,* and *enculturation.* This list is not exhaustive; other words, such as *pedagogy, instruction, direction,* and *guidance,* spring to mind. Rather, my list is illustrative of the rich ideas evocative of education.

Schooling

The word *schooling* has at least two meanings that warrant exploring. The first and literal interpretation derives etymologically from the Old English *skol,* the place where instruction takes place. In this reading, schooling is taken to be what happens in schools. Schools are the places, kinds of institutions, and environments in which a complex society (or social institution) undertakes the formal (as opposed to informal, haphazard, or incidental) instruction deemed necessary or desirable.[7] As the agent of a particular sponsoring social group or institution, the school is charged with carrying out its sponsor's wishes, accurately representing and communicating its attitudes, beliefs, values, and mores, and devising definite programs of study consistent with these expectations.

It has become customary to associate schooling more restrictively with what happens in state-operated schools modeled internationally on Western elementary and secondary state schools. These schools are typically organized into classes, governed by administrators, and taught by state-certified professional teachers according to set curricula, with stipulated times and places of instruction. Instruction is predominantly formal, laid out within the school timetable, and more or less allows extracurricular activities. Students are generally taught in teacher-directed groups. Student-initiated learning projects and tutorials for individual students are less common. School administrators, teachers, and students have clearly defined roles that evidence remarkable consistency cross-culturally.

The equation of music education with this literal interpretation of schooling constitutes the most common idea of what music education is. Historically, music has been taught in a wide variety of schools, including church schools, musical conservatories, independent music studios, private schools such as the English public schools, and commercially run music schools, and this still remains the case. However, music educators have generally associated musical schooling more restrictively with what happens in state-operated schools, particularly Western elementary and secondary state schools, and for music education programs outside the West to mirror their Western counterparts.

The word *schooling* also refers figuratively to the undergoing of some sort of discipline whereby one is "formed" or "patterned" in a particular mold desired by a particular sponsoring group, institution, or public. Students are pointed in particular directions and constrained such that their independent, hedonistic tendencies are shaped into beliefs and actions that the school public deems desirable, and they follow the paths laid out for them by their teachers. At least two contrasting approaches to this interpretation of schooling have been evident historically: a retrospective approach that finds its inspiration in the past and results in a conservative or traditional view and a prospective approach that looks to the present and future for guidance in shaping students and results in a progressive view. The former regards discipline as the corporate control and suppression of a student's personal desires; the latter sees discipline as enabling a student to fully develop her or his individual potential while also reconciling personal development with the collective needs of the group, institution, or public.[8]

The rules that the social group, institution, or society adopt to govern its operation constitute the means by which a student is guided or disciplined. They express reasoned conduct. As Israel Scheffler puts it, "Reason is always a matter of abiding by general rules or principles" that embrace conduct as well as cognition.[9] In this view, schooling is the process of becoming constrained by reason in actions as well as thoughts as one gradually comes to make the rules accepted by the public one's own.

In its defense, schooling provides an organized way of ensuring the survival of groups, institutions, and states by providing instructional environments designed to prepare students systematically for collective or social life. Especially in complex societies, the inculcation of values, beliefs, attitudes, and habits appropriate to the society are much too important to be left to happenstance; states in particular have the responsibility to provide formal, systematic instruction for students in schools.[10] Moreover, acknowledging that the knowledge included within schooling is essential implies that each subject receives serious attention.

If musical knowledge is regarded as essential to the continued survival of a group, institution, or state, a part of its cultural identity, a way of knowing, and a body of knowledge requisite for the full participation of all its members, music should form an essential part of schooling, conceived both literally and figuratively.[11] To say that music is essential in schooling does not necessarily imply that it must be regarded as equally important to other knowledge or that a particular musical subject must necessarily receive equal attention to other musical subjects. Such a simplistic view confuses the idea of importance with that of essentiality. It fails to recognize that the public may be able to prioritize knowledge in terms of the areas that seem more important than others while also recognizing all as more or less essential. And it overlooks the practical problems of identifying the corpus of knowledge considered as essential, especially at the edges, which may seem blurred or unclear.

In nineteenth-century Boston, for example, William Woodbridge argued that vocal music had a necessary place in the common school for reasons, among others, that related to its direct contribution to social life of the day.[12] As a theologian and geographer, he did not contest the supremacy of reading, writing, and arithmetic within the curriculum. Along with others who advocated the inclusion of such subjects as physiology and physical education in the common school curriculum, he sought to broaden the range of essential subjects to include vocal music (even if taught by teachers employed by musical institutions outside the common school). At this early stage of American state school education, the public disagreed about how important vocal music was.[13] Subsequent history has demonstrated that opinions about music's importance have remained divided.[14] Developments in American elementary and secondary school music during the nineteenth and twentieth centuries indicate that the school public has generally considered music to be of marginal importance at best in compulsory education and relatively unimportant when compared to other subjects such as reading and computing.

The concept of schooling as discipline is also helpful in envisaging formal music education. It draws attention to obstacles that stand in the way of music making and the means whereby a person undergoes the discipline of becoming a musician within a community of fellows.[15] An orchestral conducting teacher, for example, directs students in honing the technical and musical skills needed to become an orchestra conductor, submits them to intense critique as they gradually develop the mental concentration necessary to conceive a sonorous image of the musical work and hold it in focus throughout a performance, assists them in refining the bodily gestures necessary to communicate that image to the musicians, and demands of them the leadership skills and determination to ensure that their players express themselves personally and also comply with the group in the attainment of a corporate and an individual musical statement. A teacher's expectations of his or her students are based on a set of conducting rules observed by, and musical skills characteristic of, excellent conductors. As they undergo this process, students share a collective as well as a personal experience derived from doing similar things and submitting to a comparable critical process.

One of its most glaring flaws, however, especially when schooling is taken to be what happens in state schools, is the definition of music education in terms of incomplete objectives and elementary and intermediate levels of instruction—an unsatisfactory basis on which to build a paradigm of music education.[16] This view omits other social institutions in which music education takes place and also sees it primarily in terms of what happens during the school-age years, thereby overlooking what occurs throughout one's life. Moreover, in taking Western school music as the epitome of music education, it tends to perpetuate a parochial, culturally biased view that discounts the ways in which people make music and come to know music outside the West.

Indeed, its rule-oriented approach to discipline may result in a somewhat negative interpretation of music education, especially where discipline is viewed as control rather than as enhancement of the individual's development in the community. As such, this approach suffers from the kinds of weaknesses typical of rule-governed philosophical models of teaching generally. Although a rule-oriented music education approach need not overlook the contributions of impression and insight in shaping thought and behavior, it may be too formal and abstract a model to be taken alone.[17] Rules provide a sense of tradition and continuity, yet if viewed retrospectively rather than prospectively they may make it difficult for music education to adapt to the changing circumstances of time and place. They may constrict rather than enhance its development, thereby contributing to a discontinuity between music education and society.

Furthermore, by focusing upon formal music education, schooling may overlook the important informal dimensions of the many, often unstated yet nonetheless important ways in which one experiences the way of life of a musician. This information inheres within the actions of the social group and is either grasped intuitively or caught by, rather than being directly taught to, students. It comes from taking part in the group's activities for extended periods and in contexts that frequently have stated ends that seem irrelevant to music education. Any jazz teacher knows that she or he can only explain or show so much to a student about how to do jazz. To become an excellent player of jazz, one has to grow into it through regular participation and becoming one with other players in a community who also loves to play jazz.[18] In this respect, the jazz student faces a problem somewhat like that encountered by a person wishing to learn to play the music of another culture. For example, John Blacking describes how he attempted to play a drum to accompany a Venda woman going into a trance. After he hurried the tempo, the woman stopped and requested that he be replaced by another drummer. He had been instructed as to what to do, but he was not a Venda; "to create new Venda music," he observes, "you must *be* a Venda."[19]

Training

Training refers to the methods or ways whereby a person is taught or learns skills, know-how, or procedural knowledge, that is, how to do something, in contrast to propositional knowledge by which one "knows that" such-and-such is the case.[20] From a teacher's perspective, it is "the art of setting tasks which the pupils have not yet accomplished but are not any longer quite incapable of accomplishing."[21] Method is "a learnable way of doing something." It comprises "techniques, *modi operandi,* rules, canons, procedures, knacks, and even tricks of the trade."[22] In music, training refers specifically to how one gradually masters many things involved in music making: playing a musical instrument, singing, composing a song, analyzing the theoretical structure of a keyboard sonata, or conducting a symphony orchestra.

By skills, I follow Vernon Howard to mean a range of things, from habits and techniques to critical skills that vary in terms of their constituents and attainments, all of which can be developed through training.[23] For example, in competency-based music education, music teaching is broken down into a variety of specific skills that students are required to attain in order to be judged as competent teachers.[24] Likewise, through telling and showing, a singing teacher analyzes vocal production into its constituent skills and presents them in a carefully sequenced way that enables students to master each in turn, from the most elementary to the most advanced.[25]

Skills are governed by procedural rules that specify how certain things are to be done and when they are said to be mastered. Rules can be followed in a variety of ways, illustrated by the classification that Max Black and Howard offer. Black suggests that one may blindly master a skill without understanding how or why (rule-covered action), slavishly adhere to rules (rule-invoking action), more freely accept (rule-accepting action), or be guided by them (rule-guided action), to which Howard adds, resort to rules (rule-resorting action) in order to compare and contrast one's relative success and failure in terms of what one believes to be "their underlying causes."[26]

It is not essential that a student fully understand why or how a particular skill works in order to master it, especially at the early stages of the training process.[27] For example, a singing teacher can train a beginning student who has only a working knowledge of Italian and a reading knowledge of music to sing a simple Italian song through the use of rote teaching techniques and phonetic pronunciation of the Italian text. As a student progresses in training, however, he or she moves toward a deeper understanding of the rules and their interpretation within particular musical contexts. Black envisages the process as a loosely cyclical one in which students build on blind mastery, moving to self-conscious adherence of the rules and thence to rule-accepting, rule-guided, and (if he would allow Howard's expansion of his model) rule-resorting action and back to rule-covered behavior when one moves onto another cycle. Although my teaching experience suggests a more rhapsodic process than Black's cyclical model (even loosely envisioned) would allow, Black and Howard do a service by mapping a variety of ways in which rules govern skilled musical behavior.

Take, for example, a boy who apprentices to a concert violinist. At first he trusts his teacher implicitly, imitates her, and does exactly what she says because she is his teacher. He then begins amassing the skills needed to play the violin, and as he does he may, at first, slavishly adhere to the rules he has been given. Gradually, as he gains in confidence and ability, he comes to understand why the rules he has already internalized exist, and he accepts them as descriptors of skills he has mastered already, is guided by them more freely, and even resorts to them as ways of judging his performances.[28]

The making of violins by members of the Cremonese Guarneri family during the seventeenth and eighteenth centuries, for example, was dictated to some extent by practical experience in the curing and treatment of woods, acoustic properties inherent in the design of the instrument, and the materials and techniques for instrument varnishing.[29] This information was passed on through an apprenticeship in the family workshop from senior to junior members through several generations. They might experiment with various things (e.g., the shape, size, and position of f-holes). The limitations of the physical materials with which they were dealing, however, put certain constraints on their violin-building options and mandated that certain procedures be followed.[30]

Training is accomplished through practice. Whereas drill implies the simple mechanistic repetition of tasks allied to conditioning, practice involves the application of critical thinking and imagination as one gradually moves toward the mastery of music-making skills. This personal vision of mastery, as Howard points out, shapes the particular tasks to be undertaken.[31] They and their related purposes are ambiguous, the connections among them are contingent one upon another, and an artist must carefully attend to his or her tasks and goals in order to make corrections, adjustments, and refinements along the way. Moreover, this process tends to be open-ended rather than fixed, and the goals may change along the way, at least in the case of advanced skills. Musical or artistic skills may also be judged at various levels of excellence. As Scheffler puts it, one can at very least distinguish among "knowing how to do something," "knowing how to do it well," and "doing it brilliantly."[32]

Historically, music educators have focused on a variety of musical skills, including ear training, musical literacy, theoretical analysis, composition and improvisation, listening, and performance. The published works of Zoltán Kodály and Émile Jaques-Dalcroze in ear training and musical literacy, Paul Hindemith in theoretical analysis, Percy Scholes in music listening, and Carl Phillip Emanuel Bach in keyboard performance illustrate the many important contributions by musicians to the development of skills that comprise the doing or making of music. Each of these writers analyzed a musical skill into its component elements and carefully sequenced an approach designed so that students could master it.

For example, in his *Versuch über die wahre Art das Clavier zu spielen* (Essay on the True Art of Playing Keyboard Instruments), Bach analyzed the art of keyboard playing into three elements—"correct fingering, embellishments, and good performance"—and proceeded in Part 1 to elaborate on each in turn.[33] On fingering, after listing some general practical principles, Bach systematically described various possible fingerings for scalar passages in a variety of keys, moving consecutively through seconds, broken seconds, thirds, fourths, fifths and sixths, sevenths and octaves, and chords (three-toned, four-toned, and broken) to a discussion of more advanced principles and exceptional examples where the player must exercise personal discretion. On embellishments, after first providing some general practical principles, he cited specific instances of the appoggiatura, trill, turn, mordent, compound appoggiatura, slide, snap, and elaboration of the fermata, with musical examples of each. In a shorter treatment of performance, after dealing briefly with the question of what constitutes a good performance he moved through such specific technical matters as tempo, touch, articulation, slurs, rubato, cadenzas, and dynamics, citing examples as he went. Here, the discussion was more general than that about fingering and embellishment and built upon the material already covered. In Part 2, in likewise thorough fashion, Bach elaborated the then-common role of the keyboard player as an accompanist, discussing various skills associated with the realization of the figured bass (covering, in turn, intervals and time signatures, the rules governing the thorough bass, and other specific techniques associated with accompaniment).

Throughout his treatise, Bach laid down rules essential for what he regarded as excellent keyboard performance, being careful to note exceptions where appropriate. Some rules were treated as directives and others as guides where the performer must exercise discretion. Generally, he moved from a treatment of more basic and generally applicable rules to those that apply in specific situations or are interpreted according to the performer's discretion. His rules were also elaborated with reference to specific musical examples rather than stated as abstract principles. Because he was primarily concerned with questions of proper keyboard performance practice, Bach's rules were predominantly procedural.

In its defense, training draws from and focuses on musical practice or music making. It primarily rests on a sort of knowledge that is procedural as opposed to propositional, and because it is experiential (in that it is directly and individually experienced by the learner) and contextual (in that it occurs within a social context) it brings knowledge of self, world, and what may lie beyond that has content as well as form and can be understood as multivocal with literal and figurative dimensions.[34] As such, it directly relates to what practical musicians do—music making or, to use an old English word, musicking. It focuses on music making as a process rather than a product, a verb rather than a noun. Musical training not only yields knowledge of a certain sort but, providing it is accompanied by the development of understanding, imagination, and taste, and students undertake it voluntarily and cooperatively, the knowledge acquired also directly relates to the rest of life experience.[35]

Musical training also rests on the systematic analysis of the elements that comprise a particular music practice and the pedagogical process whereby that practice is progressively mastered. Governed by procedural rules, it is eminently reasonable. Its appeal to reason, precedent, standardized procedure, predictability, reliability, and safety, among other things, explains its widespread popularity as a way of conceptualizing instrumental and vocal music education. It is easier to follow rules as received wisdom (and one should not forget the value placed on musical traditions in which these rules find their basis) than be encumbered by the necessity of inventing ways to teach musical skills. It can also be cost-effective in its use of teacher time and effort. Standardizing approaches makes it possible to train groups as well as individuals in musical skills—an economy that is especially beneficial in the context of mass musical education.

Among its more glaring flaws, the somewhat prescriptive, teacher-directed approach in musical training emphasizes a hierarchical rather than egalitarian interrelationship between teacher and student, especially in cases of rule-covered action. Limited student input into the design of the methods employed and the ends to which they tend, and the one-way communication from teacher to student rather than two-way between teacher and student, may breed student passivity, convergent thinking, and dependence on the expectations of significant others rather than student activity, divergent thinking, and independent action. In this event, teaching reduces to a manipulative exercise of personal power over students for musical ends rather than the judicious use of influence or power with students implied in more egalitarian relationships.[36]

The conception of music education as training also drives a wedge between the theoretical and practical aspects of music and perpetuates a duality that has persisted throughout musical history. The idea that one knows more directly and experientially through doing music rather than thinking about it—that what one does constitutes primary knowledge and what one thinks about what one does is secondary knowledge—also maintains ancient philosophical dualisms between body and mind, theoretical knowledge and practice, and the physical mechanism and its ideal purpose.[37]

In giving preeminence to the practical aspects of music, training constitutes too narrow a view. It does not go far enough to emphasize propositional as well as procedural musical knowledge and therefore pays less attention to reflection, analysis, and speculation about music than is warranted.[38] Its focus on musical skills emphasizes the craft rather than the art of music—its external technique rather than the ideas that shape an artist's understanding and have primarily to do with articulating beliefs, evidence, reasons, and truth.[39]

A more holistic and wider view seeks to ally practical and theoretical aspects of music, each in tension with the other, in dialectic; the two seem not always to go together, yet they comprise distinct dimensions that enrich our understanding of music and music making. They each yield different sorts of knowledge—the one more abstract, the other more tactile and concrete—where one is not necessarily more important than, or entirely separate from, the other.[40] Such an approach effectively bridges the gap that Dewey observed in the earlier part of this century between theoretical justifications of music on the grounds of its "culture value" and a predominant emphasis on "forming technical modes of skill."[41]

Eduction

The word *eduction* means to draw out, elicit, or develop.[42] Eduction implies that a student's potential needs only to be drawn out by a teacher who skillfully arranges the external conditions such that growth and development naturally follow. Teachers are gardeners who arrange the conditions in which students, as plants, grow. The same is true, although more specifically, of music teaching and learning.

This idea has one of its fullest statements in Dewey's *Democracy and Education*.[43] Dewey maintained that the primary condition of physical growth is "immaturity." Children are both dependent upon adults and able to adapt to society; their immaturity carries a positive ability to develop habits and dispositions that enable them to interact with and adjust to their environment, and they have the potentiality or power to enlist the support of adults in this development. Thus, in Dewey's view, immaturity is not indicative that something is lacking in the child, but rather that a normal child possesses the power to become a fully functioning, mature adult within society.

Growth is not something that is done to a child. It is something that a child does. This limits what an adult may do for a child. An adult can create an environment that produces or stunts growth, however. For Dewey, experiences that produce growth are "educative," whereas those that preclude growth are "miseducative." As experiences relate to the present situation in the context of the past and their effects carry on into the future, miseducative experiences may permanently stunt or preclude a child's subsequent progress. Hence the way development is perceived is of critical importance. As in the natural world, what is not growing is decaying (in the sense that the individual is losing the power to adapt to the environment). Some teaching methods contribute to this decay, including those that rely on repetition and routines (or drill) as a way to develop habits, and it is vitally important that teachers avoid these approaches.[44]

That eduction suggests a naturalistic approach (in keeping with a student's aptitudes, attitudes, and desires) does not necessarily mean that the eductive process is simple or easy. Assumptions about human nature and potential and how eduction should proceed are rooted in theological and philosophical assumptions about the inherent goodness or evil of humanity. Dewey emphasized the importance of the environment as a causal factor in engendering personal growth and also was optimistic about human nature and the individual and collective results of education if properly carried out according to democratic ideals. By contrast to Jean-Jacques Rousseau, he held that nature and society are not inconsistent and that the claims of both can be readily reconciled within education. Although he was optimistic about the results of a naturalistic approach to education, Dewey recognized that following its principles raises a host of issues that are theoretically complex and difficult to solve in practice. These primarily have to do with designing the kinds of experiences that promote individual growth within the context of the corporate educational community.

For Dewey, growth is an end. It does not have an absolute end outside itself. The process rather than its product is of primary importance. Concepts of growth that focus on education's role as a preparation for life here or in the hereafter, as an unfolding toward some mythical state or as the training of faculties, are bound, in Dewey's view, to convey a negative and static picture of growth and perpetuate dualisms (such as those between mind and body and theory and practice). The educational process is, rather, one of "continual reorganizing, reconstructing, transforming," a life-long endeavor, and an ongoing interaction between the individual and the environment.[45]

Of the music educators to espouse the notion of eduction, possibly none is more prominent than Shinichi Suzuki. For Suzuki, "Talent is not inherited or inborn, but trained and educated."[46] Training takes place through practice, and it is this aspect that many music educators focus on—the Suzuki violin method, with its series of graded games, exercises, and pieces designed to develop such specific skills as those related to violin technique, aural memory, and ensemble playing. Suzuki views training as a part of the eductive process, one of the mechanisms through which it works.

The purpose of music education, for Suzuki, is to enrich human life. Children have potential that needs to be brought out. They naturally seek that which is good, true, and beautiful. Give them love, surround them with rich musical environments, provide them with music-making opportunities, and allow them to develop exercise patience and endurance naturally. Sooner or later their "talent" will blossom, and they will become better musicians and better people. Returning to the analogy of the seed, Suzuki wrote:

> Let's think again of the example of a tree. A seed is planted in the earth. We don't see when the germination begins. That is the doing of Mother Nature; it is the fundamental working principle. We have to wait patiently. We cannot dig the seed up to see whether it is really growing: we would just destroy everything.
>
> Suddenly a bud appears. What a joy and pleasure to watch it grow! At the same time the root, unseen in the ground, is getting stronger and has the power to produce a big sturdy tree. I think this is a good analogy for [human] ability. Once the "seed" is planted, it has to be carefully and patiently tended. Finally the "bud," or talent, presents itself and has to be educated and brought up with perseverance until the "root," or power, becomes very strong and is indissolubly tied to the personality.[47]

In its defense, the concept of eduction offers several insights. Its starting point is the student. It suggests that the study of students (particularly children) is of central importance in determining the particular pedagogical approaches to be employed. Placing students at the heart of the eductive process necessitates a knowledge of their physiological and mental development, aptitudes, attitudes, and cultural background and requires that teachers relate the subject matter to individual students so they can and do experience it directly. It is not enough for teachers to know the subject matter. They must also study students and reconcile the claims of the material with individual interests, abilities, and perspectives. Human growth and development naturally suggests that the pedagogical approaches and curricular content suitable for each developmental phase will differ significantly.[48]

As a dynamic, life-long process, eduction encompasses both early childhood and adult education. It starts from birth and continues into old age. It takes place in the school and also, importantly, especially in the early years, in the home.[49] Later, within the context of many life experiences, one continues to learn through formal and informal means within the context of various social institutions. Eduction thus becomes "coextensive with life."[50] This view of education is much wider than either schooling (with its emphasis on formal instruction, particularly of school-age children) or training (with its stress on practical skills developed in the context of formal instruction). Moreover, the role of the total environment in which people learn is recognized as an important element in the eductive process.

In eduction, students are the active agents in the learning process. They achieve understanding through personal insight. Consequently, a teacher's task shifts from being directive to assistive. Rather than actively controlling central features of the learning process, teachers become helpers in a process over which, ultimately, they have limited control. The growth metaphor clearly demonstrates these limits. No matter how carefully the environment is controlled, ultimately, learning is an individual and personal matter in which students play the key role.

The notion of teaching as assisting, helping, and caring has historically been associated with feminine roles.[51] This concept implies a collegial "I-Thou," two-way communication rather than a one-way communication between superior and subordinate. As such, it represents a different picture of teacher-student interaction than that suggested in, for example, training. One naturally helps those whom one likes, respects, or cares for. Consequently, the personal relationship between teacher and student plays an important part in the eductive process.

Envisaging music as growth resonates with philosophical and compositional thought about music and seems particularly appropriate to the concept of education in music. For example, Arnold Berleant observes that "the immediacy of the musical event reflects the directness of growth in which internal forces press forward to realize the potentialities that are inherent in the materials at hand." Although growth can be guided, he continues, "it is most successful when it works, in art as in biology, by fulfilling the possibilities that lie in the materials themselves and not by imposing external demands."[52] From a compositional perspective, Roger Sessions sees the relationship between the composer and the musical piece as "an organic one." He comments that "the conception and the composition of a piece of music are not a matter of set procedure, but a living process of growth." The "musical idea" generates a "musical train of thought" that is finally played out in the completed composition. The piece of music is therefore understood as a dynamic entity. For Sessions, "Music not only 'expresses' movement, but embodies, defines, and qualifies it."[53] It is this essential quality of musical motion and development that the growth metaphor so neatly captures.

Notwithstanding its contributions, the concept of eduction is flawed. In claiming that a student comes personally to knowledge, helped by a teacher, eduction relies on the student's "vision, or insight into meaning."[54] One explanation of how eduction occurs was offered by Augustine, who believed that teachers' words stimulate or prompt students to search for their personal understanding or vision. As Scheffler argues in reply, vision is the wrong metaphor to describe the reasoning process that undergirds knowing because it is specifically cognitive and cannot easily be stretched to cover other elements of teaching: "It provides no role for the concept of *principles,* and the associated concept of *reasons.*"[55] It gives little insight into the nature of the subject matter and how students discover the principles and rules that underlie musical theory and music making.

Eduction also draws on the metaphor of growth. Among other things, by its preoccupation with process this metaphor does not sufficiently illumine the nature of the educational product. Social processes tend to result in stable and institutionalized products. It is not enough to describe things as if they are in a continuous state of dynamic flux. One must also consider the kinds of outcomes to which processes tend. The growth metaphor is the wrong metaphor for addressing these questions.

Further, the growth metaphor cannot do justice to a range of metaphors describing aspects of the educational process: rule, community, struggle, journey, practice, conservation, consumption, and production. The growth metaphor is not comprehensive enough to convey the complexity of the educational process.

It is simplistic and inappropriate, moreover, to model educational systems on those in the natural world. The approach is tempting (and Rousseau, Dewey, Maria Montessori, and Suzuki have each used analogies from nature to explain how education works), but the analogy between social and physical events can be pressed only so far and eventually breaks down. Various systems of thought and perspectives on causation are operative and ought not to be confused with each other. Contrasting the operative time scales and the nature and complexity of events of social and physical systems respectively demonstrates how these systems differ. Social systems are appropriately examined from a variety of perspectives: physical, biological, psychological, sociological, and historical.[56] Interpreting them just from a sociological or any other single perspective and ignoring the others causes observers to fall into a reductionistic trap and fail to grasp their true complexity.[57]

The romantic vision of human nature and the optimistic view of education that characterize various formulations of eduction are problematical. The assumption that children will be motivated to learn anything if teachers present it attractively takes insufficient account of personal and social factors that cause students to choose not to cooperate in the eductive process. Dewey, Montessori, and Suzuki agreed that it is a teacher's responsibility to engender eduction. Yet students are the active agents in the educative process, and teachers are not entirely responsible for its outcome, although they are responsible for constructing an appropriate environment in which learning can take place. Students will not always turn out well if they have excellent teachers. History shows that great teachers have taught students who were unwilling to accept their ideas and became evil people.[58] We therefore need an account of education that emphasizes a student's will to learn and accounts for unmotivated, uncooperative, and rebellious students.

Nor is optimism in the effects of eduction as soundly based as its proponents would like us to believe. Dewey argued that the principal reason American democracy had not fully realized its potential lay in the failure of schools to follow democratic ideals and teachers to apply democratic principles in their classrooms. The history of American schooling, however, shows that schools, no matter how earnest their efforts and how idealistic their aims, produce some people who are unwilling to cooperate in achieving a democratic society or participating in it. Schools cannot be blamed for all of society's evils. Other operative factors—political, economic, religious, and familial—may either counteract each other or the influence of schools, thereby reducing the effectiveness of eduction.

Socialization

Socialization is the process whereby a group or institution inculcates its beliefs, values, and mores in its membership and ensures that its members continue to act in certain approved ways and hold particular shared beliefs. As such, it represents one of the social processes that characterize all groups and are essential to their survival. Without socialization, a group or institution cannot achieve and maintain a sense of unity by which members share values and expectations about how they should think and act individually and collectively.[59]

Musical socialization occurs, for example, when a choral director, wishing to build an excellent amateur choir, first teaches the initial recruits what is expected of them, and later they, in turn, instruct others by example, word, and social pressure. A case in point is Hugh Roberton's transformation of an initial group that had little knowledge of singing or performance practice from a working-class district in Glasgow, Scotland, into the Glasgow Orpheus Choir, renowned during the first part of the twentieth century.[60]

Socialization is a life-long process. It is not restricted to the young. As Henry Zentner points out, the members must be socialized and resocialized in order to bring them and keep them committed to "the subtleties of the knowledge and technique, theory and practice, and the beliefs and values which constitute the unique ideological resources and perspective of the system in purview."[61] This is evident where adults who have little musical knowledge join amateur choirs and subsequently become proficient singers, as was the case in the Glasgow Orpheus Choir. It is also the case with performing classical musicians, who must become proficient in music making and remain such throughout their lives. As they practice their art they are constantly reminded of the demands of the music performance profession and the expectations of their public, critics, and colleagues. It is not enough for them to make their triumphal debuts in major concert halls. They must continue to perform at a high level throughout their entire performing careers.

Moreover, socialization varies from one group or institution to another, from time to time, and from place to place. These differences derive from the operation of associated rules, norms, and mores that delimit the particular expectations of group members. There are significant differences in the ways in which musical socialization has operated, for example, among the Venda of South Africa, in Church of England choir schools, in the medieval music guilds of Paris and London, in the training of sitar soloists in the northern Indian classical tradition, and in contemporary Western conservatories and music schools.

Socialization takes place both formally and informally. It may include instruction by means of schooling and training, but it also extends to incidental learning gleaned by participation in the activities of the group or institution. The group's beliefs, values, and mores are taught didactically and also modeled in the context of its activities. Socialization relies extensively on informal learning in the context of group activities devoted to other ends than education, that is, in large measure, on eduction. The young are surrounded by a social environment in which they pick up knowledge through personal insight and come to adopt a set of ideas or skills as well as a way of life. This is illustrated, for example, in the education of Church of England cathedral organists in the late nineteenth century.[62] Boys were apprenticed to a cathedral organist for several years. They were taught musical theory, composition, history, and performance, individually and in small classes, and they also participated in a variety of musical events and liturgical services, living as junior members of a community of church musicians and clerics. The combination of this formal and informal instruction in the context of an environment in which they were surrounded by a group with certain beliefs, values, and practices resulted in being socialized into the way of life of a church musician.

Socialization involves persuading people that the group is important and they should remain within it and also pressuring them to maintain their commitment to it. Social pressure to conform to the corporate expectations of the group is exerted by leaders as well as its members, individually and collectively. If people believe in the importance of group membership and wish to remain within the group, the threat of expulsion from it, or the possibility of recognition by its members, provides powerful incentives for adopting its beliefs, values, and mores and acting in accordance with them. Performers in musical ensembles understand this social pressure, because the greater the prestige of the ensemble, the more its members desire to remain within it and the greater the social pressure they experience. The more prestigious the Glasgow Orpheus Choir became, for example, and the greater the competition for membership in it, the more its members desired to remain within the group and the more willing they were to embrace the artistic standards and expectations of their conductor and fellow singers and exclude those who failed to meet these standards and expectations.

Socialization is a dynamic, evolving process. It is not in a constant state of flux. Rather, it operates through, and results in, the development of stable structures that become institutionalized in mature social systems. Each group has a life-cycle, and at some phases of it (particularly in expansion and regression) the organization may be particularly change-oriented, whereas at other points (notably in maturation) it may be oriented more traditionally.[63] Because socialization contributes to and results from a group's beliefs and mores, it may be particularly progressive at some times and conservative at others. The organizational structures through which socialization operates may also change from time to time, and these may influence its content and methods.

This view of music education as socialization is taken up by John Shepherd and Graham Vulliamy in particular.[64] Shepherd observes that music teachers are caught in the midst of a culture clash in the classroom that reflects "two conflicting patterns of socialization." One represents the interests of the Western classical music establishment with which teachers identify; the other, the popular music industry with which students identify. Although they try to reduce this clash, Shepherd posits, teachers still "act as agents of social control" by applying ideas derived from Western notation uncritically and uncontextually to other musics.[65]

In its defense, socialization focuses on the social nature of knowledge. It recognizes the vested interests of groups and institutions in perpetuating certain beliefs and traditions and the role of teachers as social agents in ensuring their survival. Given the symbiotic relationship between knowledge and social institutions (that is, knowledge both reflects and impacts on them), it suggests that teachers have the twin roles of conserving institutions by transmitting ideas validated in the past and subverting them by communicating ideas oriented toward change. It implies that subject matter and instructional situation are suffused with social meaning and can only be fully understood in their social contexts; that instruction is an essentially social process whereby teacher and student interact with, relate to, and communicate with each other about subject matter (among other things); and that comparing ways of music making and approaches to musical instruction necessitates value judgments that are socially and culturally based.

Further, musical socialization extends beyond the time-span typical of schooling to include people's entire lives. In encompassing various institutions and social movements that shape the ways in which individuals come to know music, it also represents a much broader enterprise than the notions of schooling or training suggest. It includes the largely unintended, undirected, and indirect consequences of actions that turn out to be profoundly and inherently educational. Music education viewed as socialization, therefore, consists of direct formal and informal instruction and indirect instruction gleaned through participating in the way of life of a particular group or institution. The *Sacred Harp* singings in the Southeast of the United States (in which groups gather to sing from a nineteenth-century tune book), for example, are not primarily planned as educational events but as religious and social occasions. Nevertheless, they serve important educational means and enable participants to practice sight-singing skills, transmit their skills to the young, preserve the shaped-note *fasola* tradition, and foster a sense of community.[66]

The knowledge acquired is broader than either schooling and training imply, and it is also made one's own. By adopting a way of living, persons who have been musically socialized integrate musical ideas and music making, relate their musical knowledge to the gamut of ideas and activities that signify membership of the particular group or institution to which they belong, and live by those beliefs, values, and mores. For example, professional musicians possess propositional and procedural knowledge about music and also, incidentally, pick up and integrate all kinds of other understandings about life in general that will shape their life-styles. We say of them that they are musicians; they do not put on or take off the knowledge they have acquired as one does a coat. Rather, they have made the beliefs, values, and mores that characterize the musical profession their own, and their musical activities are interwoven with the rest of their lives in a holistic manner.[67]

Notwithstanding the insights it provides, because socialization primarily addresses social issues it naturally points to social rather than other sorts of explanations of phenomena. It does not focus on music as music. Nor may it take sufficient account of related anthropological, cultural, historical, philosophical, and theological issues among those that arise within the context of musical events and warrant other sorts of explanations. The Marxist view of music making solely in terms of ideological clashes between social classes is reductionistic and simplistic, for example, precisely because it fails to take into account other systems of thought and approaches to causation.[68] Consequently, Shepherd and Vulliamy are careful to insist that sociological explanations of musical events provide only part of the picture and must be supplemented by other interpretations.[69]

Being institution-specific, socialization cannot encompass the sorts of problems that arise for music education when one institution's beliefs, values, and mores come into conflict with those of another (as in Shepherd's analysis of contemporary Western classrooms when two patterns of socialization under the aegis of the political establishment and the popular music industry clash with each other). Socialization can tell us how each institution transmits musical ideas and practices; it can also illuminate how these systems of thought and practice differ. It cannot, however, show us how we should reconcile them within the wider cultural and human situation.

Socialization may seem to suggest an extreme form of relativism that renders comparisons among different instances of music making tenuous or invalid. On the contrary, however, some general, culturally based, characteristics of world musics may permit useful comparisons among instances of music making, although these may be of a different sort than the formal criteria offered in the past. Among these criteria one might include such things as the degree to which this instance of music fulfills its culture-specific rules; its ability to accomplish what it is supposed to do (e.g., incite to dance, accompany the onset of trance, induce profound calm, and intrigue intellectual contemplation); and the extent to which it reflects the underlying ethical values of participants.[70] Suppose, however, that having specified our values with respect to gender relationships, particularly sexual abuse, we then make comparisons among certain rock lyrics and opera texts in respect of instances of abusive attitudes and behaviors and assign relative ethical values to the textual material. The origin of these ethical values is social as well as theological, philosophical, and psychological. Unless we engage in reductionist thinking, therefore, socialization presents an insoluble problem.

Enculturation

Historically, the word *enculturation* has had two meanings, one anthropological and the other idealistic. The first draws on anthropological ideas of culture as the totality or compendium of life—as Dewey puts it, its "customs, institutions, beliefs, victories and defeats, recreations and occupations."[71] In this sense, enculturation refers to the life-long process whereby people acquire a personal and collective cultural identity as humans—a way of life individually experienced and corporately shared within the context of a particular sociocultural group or society in which they live. The second draws on idealistic, even utopian, views of culture as that toward which humanity strives. As Werner Jaeger shows, the Greek notion of *paideia* embodied ideals of human beings as they ought to be and implied educating people into their "true form, the real and genuine human nature" characterized by such qualities of heroism, beauty, justice, and self-sacrificing patriotism.[72]

Although he took an anthropological view of culture, Dewey also implied the existence of ideals when he described culture as "something cultivated, something ripened" (as "opposed to the raw and crude"), "something personal," "cultivation with respect to appreciation of ideas and art and broad human interests," and "the capacity for continually expanding the range and accuracy of one's perception of meanings."[73] He did not, however, take sufficient account of the repressive elements within society that can militate against the realization of these ideals. Paulo Freire went further than Dewey to conceive of education as "an ideal and a referent for change in the service of a new kind of society."[74] Pedagogy "cannot do without a vision of [humanity] and of the world."[75] Its essence is properly one of humanizing and liberating people from all forms of repression, challenging and enabling them to transform their world into a just and compassionate society.

My view of enculturation recognizes the tension between these anthropological and idealistic views and attempts, somewhat paradoxically, to meld aspects of them. Culture has realistic as well as idealistic elements. Anthropological notions describe what culture has been and now is; idealistic perspectives provide insights into potentialities—what culture might have been and could become. Although the ideals pursued in modern times may be more diverse in their specific cultural manifestations than those implicit in the idea of *paideia* (for the modern world presents a far greater complexity than a Homer, Hesiod, or Tyrtaeus might have known), ideals are nevertheless part and parcel of the process whereby people become independent, fulfilled, and, ultimately, citizens of the world.

Enculturation may be likened, then, to a series of concentric circles representing progressively more inclusive understandings and extending outward from a particular culture to encompass a global view of humanity. It delineates the status quo and potentially encapsulates a transformative quality of making what now is into something better. As such, it may also be described in terms of elusive ideals and linked integrally to value judgments and normative considerations, those of what should be as well as what is. To acquire culture, in this view, is ultimately to gain a wider knowledge than the foregoing notions of schooling, training, eduction, or socialization imply.

Enculturation involves two sometimes conflicting processes—transmission and acculturation—the first emphasizing tradition and the second underscoring change. Transmission describes the acquiring of culture through the passage of wisdom from one generation to another. Wisdom consists of myths, rituals, values, and understandings that have been collected in the past; regarded as definitive or representative of particular groups, institutions, or cultures; and valued to such an extent that they are transmitted from generation to generation. It contains what is believed to be true, of intrinsic and extrinsic worth, and deserving of preservation. It is not fragmentary knowledge, but that which brings a sense of unity, wholeness, and organizing principle to knowledge of self, world, and what lies beyond, as Alfred North Whitehead put it, "the way in which knowledge is held."[76] It is shown by a holistic grasp or understanding of a body of knowledge and its significance to the rest of life experience. A person might be socialized as a performing musician into certain beliefs, mores, and practices and still not be enculturated if she or he has not acquired a wider sense of cultural identity and wisdom.[77]

Moreover, culture is not something fixed and immutable for all time. It is in the process of dynamic change and at sometimes less change-oriented than at others. Like all social systems, culture tends to become more or less institutionalized and canonized. It is product as well as process. As the social institutions of which they are a part, for example, ways of music making tend to become somewhat fixed, institutionalized, and regarded as traditional. They come to comprise bodies of musical wisdom that are valued and preserved. Enculturation, then, is the process whereby people come to understand this musical "wisdom" and appropriate it for themselves.

Musical enculturation implies understanding the place of music in and through culture and also culture in and through music. To come to understand one's culture is to acquire wisdom, a holistic grasp of an important body of knowledge and an understanding of the interrelationships among one aspect and another. It is not enough, therefore, to study music by analyzing and performing particular musical works. One must also understand, among other things, the social, political, economic, philosophical, artistic, religious, and familial contexts in which music making occurs. This view commits me to a contextual and interdisciplinary approach to music and the integration of this knowledge with the rest of life experience. It also suggests, paradoxically, that music making is the means as well as the end of enculturation and enculturation is the means as well as the end of music making.

Like socialization, enculturation is accomplished through direct instruction and participation in the rituals of music making. Jacques Attali views the continued repetition of music through electronic recording and playback as the exercise of power to silence people and a hindrance to music making.[78] It is only through opportunities that allow people to create music (as well as perform it), he suggests, that this tyranny can be broken. Kivy concurs that music-making rituals are presently in danger of being destroyed by the impact of technological invention. In order to preserve them, he argues, people should actively participate as music-makers rather than just passive listeners.[79]

I am not satisfied, however, that technological invention is the villain in this piece.[80] Doubtless some musical rituals are being destroyed, but others are being created to replace them; this is only to be expected if one allows that musical rituals change from time to time. Nor need listening be a passive experience. As Scholes reminds us, listening can and ought to be an active participatory process.[81] Whatever the specific nature of musical rituals, however, they rely upon preserving a vital sense of participation in music making through such activities as improvisation and composition, performance, and listening.

Thus far, I have referred to enculturation as if only one set of cultural beliefs, values, and practices is involved in the process. Although this might have been true throughout history, the situation is now more complex. Subcultures of multicultural societies interact; some are relatively dominant and others comparatively subordinate. Relative dominance over others is influenced, among other things, by political, religious, economic, and social factors. Within a given society, patterns of socialization associated with various societal institutions may result in tensions and conflicts. Some values clash with others—freedom with oppression, equality with inequality, and community with isolation. As people who have been oppressed, excluded, and otherwise silenced come to understand the possibilities for justice and a sense of community, they are forced to reexamine and even revolutionize their beliefs and practices and those of their oppressors if possible.[82]

"Acculturation" describes the acquiring of culture in situations of culture contact. The word *acculturation* has been defined anthropologically, for example, by Melville Herskovits, as the process whereby "isolated traditions or considerable blocs of custom are passed on by one human group to another; by means of which a people adapt themselves to what has been newly introduced and to the consequent reshuffling of their traditions as these were aligned before the new elements were presented," with the added proviso that there is "historic control" over the "situations of contact."[83] Herskovits's definition suggests that musical acculturation occurs when different musical traditions come into contact with each other under some element of historical control and a change or reorganization of a group's musical traditions (its belief systems and practices) results from that culture contact. Rather than using the word *acculturation* in its strictly anthropological sense, however, I prefer to describe it more broadly, also admitting the possibility of idealistic conceptions of culture where certain ideals are held to be more or less universalistic and normative and color the acculturative process.

Examples of musical acculturation include the adoption of Western country music by Native Americans as part of their lives and the acceptance of the musical values of music teachers trained in the Western classical tradition—representing the dominant subculture—by school students who are well versed in rock music, the politically subordinate subculture.[84] Musical traditions of whatever sort—Native American, Western country, classical, or rock—involve divergent yet interrelated sets of beliefs, values, and rituals transmitted through such institutions as the family, mass media, and the classical music profession. A group chooses either to adapt or assimilate another music (or parts of it) within its own musical culture or abandon its tradition for a new one, depending on the compatibility of the traditions, the political and economic power of proponents of the new tradition to force its acquiescence, and other circumstances under which contact takes place. Consequently, acculturation may result in changes in musical traditions or the loss of musical traditions due to the power and force of particular musical traditions to absorb or supplant others. Whatever the particular outcome of the contact, if group members (individually and collectively) are to achieve and maintain a sense of their cultural identity, acculturation necessitates that they somehow respond to similar, divergent, and conflicting values, beliefs, and rituals associated with other musical traditions that are not their own or with which they have not been identified.

In its defense, enculturation potentially provides a worldview of music education consistent with some of the principles I have described as the "second view" of music education. Allowing the possibility that certain ideals may be held to be more or less universalistic (even though they might be realized in diverse ways), enculturation permits and encourages internationalistic and contextual perspectives that take account of multicultural societies. As a life-long process, it includes the various social groups and institutions in which music making takes place. Further, its relativistic approach to musical traditions and the ways by which people come to know music (and its recognition of the need to accommodate or reconcile competing and conflicting approaches) avoids cultural chauvinism or imperialism and necessitates and facilitates dispassionate comparisons among musical traditions and approaches to music education.

The knowledge enculturation brings is potentially holistic and broad. By taking account of the interrelationship of culture and music, it facilitates the development of musical skills, cultural understandings, and a deeper awareness of self, world, and whatever lies beyond. Like socialization, by including incidental, indirect, and informal instruction (through participation in rituals) as well as planned, direct, and formal instruction, it constitutes a liberal understanding of the scope and nature of musical instruction.

Enculturation offers the prospect of a multifaceted and multidisciplinary view of music education couched at a high level of generality. It highlights music's functional role as a facet of the individual and collective sense of cultural identity, whether of a particular culture or humanity in general. As such, it envisages music making within a social context and links practice and theory by drawing attention to the mythologies and belief systems underlying practice. By virtue of the fact that it encompasses various systems of understanding and approaches to causation, music education conceived as enculturation invites interdisciplinary study by such researchers as anthropologists, physiologists, psychologists, sociologists, historians, geographers, philosophers, theologians, musicians, and educators.

Notwithstanding these insights, the concept of enculturation has several detractions. Some would argue that it is not sufficiently exclusive; it includes much that is unplanned, indirect, and incidental in the context of activities with other than educational ends. They may wish to include within education only those activities that are planned as educational.[85] Most social actions, however, have unintended and unanticipated consequences. Social occasions may serve central or ancillary educational purposes, even if there is not a conscious or stated educational intention. As my earlier example of the *Sacred Harp* singings illustrates, activities not planned as such may turn out to exemplify educational means and ends. From a practical viewpoint, it is easier to make inferences on the basis of the nature of the activities engaged in and their results than on intentions, stated or otherwise. Others, like Giovani Gentile, may prefer to distinguish between education and enculturation, taking an idealistic and more limited view of education that has "knowledge for its end" in contrast to enculturation, which has a nationalistic "way of life" as its goal.[86] Such distinctions, however, sometimes either amount to rationalizations for a bias toward Western learning or involve unduly narrow conceptions of education.[87]

The complexity and ambiguity of the word *culture,* referring simultaneously to particular cultural groups and the whole of human culture, conceived as process and product and construed in an anthropological as well as idealistic sense, creates another potential problem. If the notion of culture is ambiguous and complex, so, too, are the means and ends of enculturation. On the other hand, this complexity and ambiguity may enrich our understanding of enculturation by permitting a narrow focus on particular cultures or cultural groups at some times during the enculturative process and a broad, international, and historical focus within the context of practical and idealistic considerations. Music educators may choose to ensure that students first acquire a sense of their musical roots by studying the music of their place and people, for example. Thereafter, they might gradually introduce them to other world musics within their respective social, political, economic, and religious contexts, believing that this approach enables students to grasp important interrelationships between music and life and understand the inherent worth of diverse music traditions, especially to the people whose identities are bound up in them.

Rather than surrender or soft-pedal idealistic notions of musical beliefs and practices, music educators are also faced with reconciling the tensions between idealistic perspectives (which may be internationalistic and favor classical musical traditions) and realistic perspectives (which may be localistic and emphasize folk music traditions) within the music curriculum. That such a reconciliation is not always possible points up the inherent contradictions and tensions in the educational enterprise.[88]

Like socialization, enculturation does not shed much light on the source of associated psychological, philosophical, theological, ethical, religious, and musical understandings. Although it is true that these other ways of knowing are closely interrelated with human nature and society, they are also understood in their own terms. Throughout this chapter, for example, I have laid aside questions relating to the nature of music, allowing a social definition of music to stand. This, however, is too simplistic a view. Music is understood formally as well as contextually. Enculturation can help provide a contextual understanding of music, but it cannot do justice to its formal aspects. Distinctively musical perspectives are also needed. I referred earlier to the possibility that acculturation can result either in invalidating or supplanting musical traditions or in validating and enriching them. Normative decisions about what acculturation should accomplish are defended with respect to moral and ethical values, and these ultimately lie outside the purview of enculturation. Additional philosophical and theological insights, among others, are therefore necessary.

Implications

In this chapter I have explored several ways of conceptualizing music education: schooling, training, eduction, socialization, and enculturation. Each contributes to our understanding but is lacking in one respect or another. The broadest notion—enculturation—although potentially subsuming the others, because it omits other grounded perspectives, provides only partial insight into music education. In conjunction with these other views, however, it suggests something of the complexity of the process by which people come to know music.

The multiplicity of perspectives on the educational process, and the limitations of each when taken alone, suggests that dialectical tensions must be resolved. Within each of the foregoing concepts of education are further dialectics requiring solution. Although that prospect complicates the notion of education, it also enriches our understanding of its many aspects. Viewing education as a multifaceted and problematical enterprise fraught with challenges necessitates settling what are sometimes seemingly impossible tensions. Yet music education policymakers must find some resolution, however temporary or partial.

Schooling, training, eduction, socialization, and enculturation articulate, when taken together, at least a part of a broad view of music education. That view goes beyond the traditional concept equated with school music and includes the activities of other societal institutions. It also implies life-long musical learning, from babyhood and young childhood through the various stages of adult life to old age, encompassing everything from the most elementary through the most advanced levels of instruction. As such, the objectives of music education are necessarily broad, complex, and include many activities beyond the traditional focus of music educators. Rather than seeing their role as providing a limited range of musical knowledge and skills, they must see themselves engaged in an enterprise that integrates music with the rest of life.

This view suggests, in addition, a range of issues that touch on the way music educators do their work. For example, music as taught in schools is often decontextualized and cut off from musical and social contexts in the rest of life. Students, stripped of their need to earn a living through music, may sometimes be disinterested in their musical studies as a result. They do not recognize how the information they are learning relates to the rest of their lives and why they need to know the material. This has not always been the case. Historically, music apprentices needed certain knowledge in order to earn a living at music making. The need to make a living was a powerful incentive for their learning. Through socialization and enculturation they were prepared not just with musical information but to participate in a way of life as musicians. If music education were to be reconstrued to include socialization or enculturation, musical learning would have to be more contextualized than it now is, and students, like their apprentice counterparts, would be more motivated to learn. Applying the principles underlying musical apprenticeship to school music, then, would broaden the objectives of musical instruction and also alter its methods fundamentally.

Reconciling dialectics among the various conceptions of education suggests that education is a complicated affair and implies that music education policymakers must balance competing and conflicting interests, some of which seem irreconcilable. In the view I have presented in this chapter, no one concept of education suffices. Each has strengths and limitations. What remains is to find out how to make a reciprocity among these various visions of education and to accept the ambiguities, tensions, and even conflicts that necessarily result.

No wonder that from time immemorial philosophers and many of the brightest minds have grappled with educational problems of one sort or another. The fact that education seems, superficially, to be very simple and practical and yet, upon closer inspection, turns out to be immensely problematical and even theoretical would be reason enough for their interest. Indeed, the intractability of the educational problems encountered and the human condition underlying them could explain this widespread interest in education. Yet educators cannot stop at articulating and critiquing ideas. They must ultimately apply their beliefs, values, and mores to the particular situations in which they work. Practice turns out to be just as complicated as the world of ideas from which it draws and to which it contributes. Like their philosopher counterparts, practitioners must reconcile disparate visions and balance competing interests, many of which defy resolution. This is anything but a simple task. Instead, it requires wisdom, imagination, daring, verve, and resilience among a host of other qualities necessary to engage the philosophical and practical tasks and challenges of music education.

Although complicating the task of education, as I have done in this chapter, I am also entrusting music educators with making the necessary judgments to pass on musical wisdom from one generation to the next. To do this effectively entails thinking critically about how to reconcile and prioritize these visions of education and how to translate this "mix" of visions into practical reality. Ultimately, such decisions are a matter of personal as well as corporate reflection, forged within the context of particular instructional situations. They cannot be reduced to simple formulas but must be considered and applied by the music education community in the light of prevailing circumstances of a given time and place.

At the outset of this chapter I deliberately laid aside questions about the nature of music and chose, first, to focus my attention on various facets of education. My choice of this ordering of questions was partly guided by my hunch that the question of what music is may be more difficult and complicated than that of what constitutes education. It seemed better to take the simpler problem first. Notwithstanding its challenges, however, the nature of music must be of central concern to music educators and those interested in their work, and I next turn to the question of what is music.

On Spheres of Musical Validity

One of the intriguing aspects of music is the great variety of musical traditions, ways of music making, and transmitting musical knowledge from one generation to another evident historically and internationally. Why do so many musics coexist, each with a public that identifies with that music and whose culture is partly defined by it? Can this diversity be explained in a way that permits a global and context-sensitive view of world musics? How do these musical traditions maintain themselves, especially in the face of competition or opposition from others? These, among other questions, are especially relevant to music educators whose objective includes musical enculturation.

Francis Sparshott has written that "we should be prepared to find that different musical practices, or different aspects of one practice, answer to different kinds of interest, and that some or all of these interests might be specific interests in music and in nothing else." He continues, "It may turn out that the musics of the world are the way they are because that is the way people want them, and the reason they want them that way is because, in each case, the music is just what it is."[1] Sparshott's suggestion seems well-taken. We cannot leave the matter rest in a tautology, however: X is so because Y; Y is so because X. Quite apart from its logical problems, Sparshott's statement does not illuminate the nature of social and musical change and the role of music education within the music-making process. Rather, questions relating to the nature of the interrelationship between music and society, how social expectations of music arise, and how music, in turn, feeds social expectations merit some explanation.

Three assumptions undergird the following analysis. First, "theoretical types" (sometimes called "ideal types") provide ways whereby musical and social events can be conceptualized; their use is well established in the social sciences.[2] Musicologists have also employed them to distinguish musical styles and historical epochs in music.[3] Theoretical types organize many specific events by means of a manageable array of conceptual constructs or categories from which generalizations about other related events can more or less be made. They provide models, or ways of looking at the phenomenal world that are both literal and figurative, but they should not be confused with the world itself.

Theoretical types are culturally and historically relative and as such compare one with another; they consist of several "analytically abstract and conceptually independent categories of phenomena" that may be translated to a set of conceptual common denominators; they point in logically opposite directions while being inextricably linked and as such are in tension rather than unity; they are capable of conversion to some sort of metric, even if it is a crude index rather than precise measure; they may be conceptually distinguished from empirical types that arise primarily from empirical observations in the phenomenal world, although the two may be practically indistinguishable; and their validity and reliability can be assessed by means of logical and moral tests.[4]

Second, musical events have historically been examined from a social perspective in two principal ways: first, through an analysis of their structures and functions (for instance, Theodor Adorno's taxonomy of music listeners and Alphons Silbermann's classification of structures and functions in musical groups) and, second, by focusing on the meanings and symbols inherent in musical events through an examination of their social processes (for example, Paul Honigsheim's description of social processes in music).[5] Both approaches are useful and yield different insights into musical events, much like the differences between still photographs and moving pictures.

A practical way of reconciling or melding aspects of these different approaches has been shown by Honigsheim, who analyzed the structures and functions within each of the social processes he identified. In his study of the process of musical sponsorship, for example, he described various structurally and functionally grounded categories, such as the influence of religious leaders, royalty, nobility, private individuals, impresarios and agents, and schools.[6] One might also take the opposite approach of analyzing processes within a structural-functional framework.

Third, music is interrelated with society in multifaceted ways. Of these ways, several tensions seem particularly important. Music is both related to and independent of the other arts. The ancient Greeks thought of music as encompassing poetry, song, dance, drama, and instrumental music. Subsequent specialization in the arts led Western classical musicians to think of music in a much narrower sense, as a separate art form. In *Philosophy in a New Key,* however, Susanne Langer draws attention to the commonalities among music, drama, poetry, dance, myth, and rite, among other nondiscursive ways of knowing. She fails to underscore the role of social context in sufficiently understanding musical meaning, yet her analysis of music as closely related to the arts, myth, and religion opens the way for others to explore how music is similar to and different from other ways of knowing. In so doing, she reminds readers that vestiges of an earlier time remain. Music is thought of restrictively and independently of other arts in the abstract instrumental music of a Beethoven symphony; it is also thought of broadly and integratively with other arts in a Wagner opera or Tchaikovsky ballet. So important is the total arts concept of music that opera is regarded as one of the great triumphs of Western music.[7]

Music has form and function. "Form" refers to articulated structure that relies on the skills of the composer, performer, and listener to make and apprehend. "Function" means the use music serves. Philosophers of music have largely overlooked social aspects of musical form and function until recently, when various writers argued that music making is fundamentally a matter of practices motivated and constrained by, and understood within, particular social and cultural contexts.[8] Many world musics are integrated arts that serve myth and rite or mark particular social and political calendars. Rather than being means to their own ends, these musics constitute means to other ends, such as the maintenance of the societal structures and processes in which they are found. In the past, rules undergirding Western classical music have been applied indiscriminately to an analysis of the structure and function of all musics. We now recognize that Western norms do not apply to all musics universally, but that many rules govern particular musics. Each must be understood in its own terms, formally and functionally.

Music is a part of society, and musical structures reflect and exemplify social structures. During the past half-century, writers from the social sciences and humanities have advanced the notion of an intimate and intrinsic relationship between music and society.[9] They have argued that music is suffused with meaning that is musically and culturally interpreted and that it contributes in important ways to a sense of shared social consciousness that characterizes a given society. Blacking, for example, has contrasted Western classical music, which reflects Western hierarchical social structures and mores and values individualism and competition, with the indigenous music of the Venda people of South Africa, which reveals egalitarian social values and beliefs and values communalism and cooperation. He believes that music cannot be prophetic of society, but only follow it. On the contrary, the reciprocal interaction between society and music is dynamic; music not only follows society but also impacts, portends, and even constructs and reconstructs it. As such, music making involves a dialectic between social conservation and reconstruction.[10]

Music is corporately and individually understood. It is limited to, and transcends, cultural context. Earlier this century, Charles Ives suggested that the reason for this paradox lay in music's possession of both substance and manner: substance is imaginatively grasped in the musical content, and manner is indicated in its style. It is music's substance that enables it to transcend a particular time and place.[11] Substance and manner are inextricably intertwined. Nevertheless, the conceptual distinction between them highlights the importance of, and differences between, personal and social perspectives on music.

Substance, noted Ives, is grasped individually; manner is understood in terms of social expectations. Substance permits music to reach beyond its time and place; manner ties it to a particular time and place. Taken figuratively, a Bach partita seems just as fresh and relevant today as it did three centuries ago and a Japanese *koto* ensemble moves an English as well as Japanese audience because of the presence of musical substance, or that which intrigues the imagination more or less independently of the listener's cultural understandings of the music. Listeners can fully understand the partita or the *koto* performance, however, only as they also grasp its manner, its stylistic and contextual aspects. Recognizing the complementary nature of these personal and social understandings about music highlights the importance of studying the interrelationship of music and society from a variety of perspectives, be they social, religious, musical, philosophical, psychological, or physiological.

Some theoretical tools are necessary to examine questions relating to the formation and maintenance of diverse musical traditions, the existence of publics within them, and the related challenges for music education. One such tool is provided by adapting the concept of "sphere of musical validity" originally formulated by Georg Simmel and elaborated by Peter Etzkorn.[12] Spheres of musical validity tend to arise in at least five ways, and each process (construed as a theoretical type) tends to focus on the activities of a particular institution or segment of society.

The Nature of Spheres of Musical Validity

Etzkorn observes that a sphere of social validity in art arises when "similar cognitive responses or meanings are evoked through a shared symbolism communicated" by it.[13] Restated, a sphere of musical validity exists about a given musical genre, style, or tradition when similar cognitive responses or meanings are evoked through a shared symbolism that it communicates. This statement is problematical. It is ambiguous with respect to the level of generality at which the sphere of musical validity should be cast, and it takes a narrow view of intellection that seems to exclude musical feeling, emotion, and corporeality.

That there should be ambiguity in the notion of a sphere of musical validity is interesting because it permits an examination of musical groups at different levels of generality. Jazz, construed as a genre, for example, could be considered a sphere of musical validity. More specifically, there are different instances of jazz—bebop, blues, and so on—suggesting different sorts of jazz or different spheres of musical validity. One sphere of musical validity called jazz dissolves into several spheres called bebop, blues, and so forth. Seen in comparative terms, then, jazz can be compared with classical music, or bebop with blues.

On the matter of intellection, it is important to recast the definition of spheres of musical validity more broadly than Etzkorn and state that similar cognitive, emotional, and physical understandings are communicated through a given musical event. The meanings conveyed, symbolisms grasped, and responses evoked are construed as beliefs, attitudes, understandings, feelings, and sensory and bodily impressions. These feelings and understandings are played out in actions and practices, moreover. Thus, when people make music, they do so within a community of those who share attitudes, understandings, and practical traditions. This community acts as any social group, corporately and individually, and assumes and maintains a life of its own.

A sphere of musical validity is both inclusive and exclusive. It is inclusive in that the individuals within it hold shared beliefs, opinions, and mores and act in certain prescribed and proscribed ways according to given expectations shared by a musical group. It is exclusive in that individuals and groups outside the sphere who do not share these beliefs and expectations are excluded from membership in it. One has either to be born within a particular group or society or be instructed or inducted into that set of beliefs, values, and mores from the outside. One may grow up within a particular environment and absorb certain understandings and expectations through a kind of osmosis thought of as eduction; be formally instructed, schooled, or trained in particular ways of thinking and acting; or otherwise be socialized or enculturated into given sets of beliefs and expectations characteristic of particular groups or social institutions.

The common understanding shared by the community comprising a sphere of musical validity is described in a different context by Immanuel Kant in *Critique of Aesthetic Judgement* as *sensus communis,* an individual's judgment that others *ought* to agree with her or him.[14] Although Kant was speaking universally and with specific reference to questions of taste and estimations of what is beautiful, his description of this common understanding seems an apt way of conceptualizing what occurs within a sphere of musical validity. He commented, "The judgement of taste exacts agreement from every one; and a person who describes something as beautiful insists that everyone *ought* to give the object in questions his [or her] approval and follow suit in describing it as beautiful."[15]

For Kant, taste is a kind of common or public sense in which one presumes to ascribe the judgments others ought to make regarding a particular thing of beauty. Applied to judgments of rightness and goodness within a particular sphere of musical validity, Kant's concept of *sensus communis* captures the corporate as well as individual understanding of music. Individuals within a given sphere of musical validity have the collective sense that particular rules must be satisfied in order for a musical event to be appropriate or exemplary. They act on the basis of these expectations and expect others to do likewise.

Various sociologists have posited a notion of groups formed about shared musical understandings and ways of music making. Silbermann, for example, bases his analysis of the sociology of music around the "musical experience," or the act of making music. He proposes a reciprocal relationship between the musical experience of the composer, performer, and listener such that sociomusical groups form about these musical experiences. Each group is a " 'collection of individuals who are connected with one another through positive complementary social relationships' " in the context of

musical events and " 'distinguishable from all other such collections of individuals.' "[16] Others have suggested that a sociomusical group is characterized by a "mentality" or "mode of mental conduct which characterizes some
social collectivity that holds it in common."[17] I find this view too narrow
because it excludes, among other things, rituals and other corporate activities that bind the group together.

What makes these shared understandings possible are sets of rules governing and exemplifying musical ideas and practices based on commonly
understood symbol systems. Whether the objective of a particular musical
event is to arouse people to dance, trance state, or patriotic fervor, the
significance of the event is grasped intellectually, emotionally, and physically by the participants in it. Whether it be an operatic performance, a rock
concert, or a corroboree, the community of the initiated comprehends its
significance cognitively, affectively, and corporeally. This view of understanding is a broad and holistic one that encompasses reason, intuition,
imagination, feeling, and sense. The rules are understood from a variety of
perspectives, moreover, reflecting the different viewpoints of the actors in
the process. How one understands a particular operatic performance, for
example, depends on whether one is its composer, singer, dancer, conductor, designer, stage manager, instrumentalist, lighting technician, or patron.
And the same is true of a rock concert or a corroboree. Examining a given
sphere of musical validity more closely, therefore, may reveal a variety of
subgroups—spheres within spheres—each more or less sharing common
elements with the others.

Musical events evoke meanings that are individually and collectively
apprehended; they also articulate and reinforce the group identity, which, in
turn, is exemplified in and reinforces its musical expression in an ongoing,
interactive process. In this open, dynamic, system, where particular musical
practices reflect, reinforce, and reconstruct a given social community, musical ideas and practices can be both antecedent to, and consequent of, that
community. Spheres of musical validity refer literally and figuratively to
musical communities, shared beliefs, attitudes, and mores. This ambiguity
provides for a rich interpretation of these spheres as they apply to the study
of world musics and their publics and suggests that they are appropriately
studied from interdisciplinary perspectives.

Spheres of musical validity may be more or less contiguous with a particular culture, constitute one of several subcultures, or extend over several
cultures. Examples of unitary cultures are rare; one typically encounters
several spheres of musical validity within a particular culture or a sphere of

musical validity extending over several cultures. For example, Wilfrid Mellers has suggested that the musical culture in medieval England was more homogeneous than it is now. Then, art and popular music, sacred and secular music, were essentially united in that they related to the feudal order in which "cleric and peasant mutually succoured each other, one providing for the needs of the body, the other for the needs of the soul."[18] Now, music and musical expression have become much more fragmented. Sidney Finkelstein has described the close ties between folk music and music in the Western classical tradition, especially during the seventeenth and eighteenth centuries, and their escalating, gradual breakdown during the nineteenth and twentieth as many composers retreated from an active commentary on, and direct challenge to, society.[19] The present multiplicity of spheres of musical validity in tension, competition, or conflict, and the internationally pervasive nature of some musics, no doubt is the result of such developments as the industrialization of Western societies, imperialist expansion by European powers, explosion of technological and scientific knowledge, developments in international trade and migration on a scale unprecedented in recorded history, and the internationalization of the music industry through mass communication technology and global marketing strategies.

Like all social groups, spheres of musical validity tend to become institutionalized and self-perpetuating as each community seeks to maintain itself in time and place. Musical groups may coalesce to form musical subcultures or cultures or dissolve into smaller entities. They may cooperate or compete with each other, matching or clashing with the mores prevalent in a given society. Individuals within a particular sphere of musical validity may tend to adopt musical mores that change more slowly than musical fashion, believing that their particular beliefs and actions are superior to others not within their sphere.[20] Consequently, communication difficulties and conflicts arise among individuals, groups, subcultures, or cultures.

Spheres of musical validity also differ in regard to their social networks. Robert Stebbins has described the morphological and interactional characteristics of the social networks of amateur musicians.[21] His approach illustrates one way of describing the dimensions or size of a sphere of musical validity in geographic or spatial terms, the intensity of relationships within a given musical group, and the sorts of social networks that are established and maintained. These social networks help explain the dynamic character of spheres of validity and contribute to their state of continual becoming.

Individuals may be members of several spheres of musical validity simultaneously and in different relationship to each sphere.[22] Some spheres depict different musical tastes, for example, country music and African American gospel music, and others characterize different functions, for example, formal ceremonial music of public occasions and informal music making in the home. Alternatively, individuals can be positioned differently within several spheres of musical validity. At the center of the sphere of musical validity are those whose life-style is symbolized and integrated by a particular music; at its periphery are those whose connections with it are looser, for example, people who may prefer this music over others in which they participate but who might easily move from this sphere to another. In some cases several spheres partly overlap because of certain common aspects, for example, gospel and country music. Others seem opposed and entirely separate, illustrated by the antipathy of some classical musicians to jazz and rock or vice versa. Even where spheres of musical validity seem to be entirely separate or in opposition, as with some twentieth-century classical and popular music, they overlap in some instances, for example, in Leonard Bernstein's *Mass, West Side Story,* and *On the Waterfront* suite, Andrew Lloyd Webber's *Requiem* and *Phantom of the Opera,* and Paul Simon's *Graceland* and *Rhythm of the Saints* recordings.

Some spheres of musical validity composed of individuals and groups who constitute the establishment may become more powerful than others that may be considered subversive and anti-establishment. These less politically powerful musical traditions may be ignored, ostracized, and suppressed by more powerful elements in society despite the fact that they may have pervasively popular appeal. The Western classical music profession, for example, has historically considered domestic music making (associated particularly with amateurs, women, and children) to be less important than that associated with formal rituals and ceremonies (in which men have traditionally played the principal roles, often as professionals). It has largely ignored such music as *hausmusik, gebrauchsmusik,* or, as Paul Hindemith preferred, *sing- und spielmusik.*[23]

In a multicultural society in which various spheres of musical validity coexist, the question of whose music is to be taught in state-supported schools has political and musical ramifications and important policy implications: Should school music be characterized by musical pluralism or monism? Will the views of the cultural establishment be taught exclusively, or will other musical perspectives be included? and Which particular musics shall be incorporated within the curriculum? The tendency to exclude or deemphasize musics of ethnic minorities and some forms of popular music in favor of Western classical music in Western school curricula illustrates how music teaching tends to ensure the social and cultural reproduction of the Establishment and maintain the status quo insofar as ethnic and social stratification is concerned.

Spheres of musical validity exist within a sociocultural context and are affected, in particular, by the societal orientation toward change or tradition; these sociocultural and global influences may affect their number and nature at any given time. In this regard, Pitirim Sorokin has postulated two theoretical types between which societies oscillate: the sensate phase oriented toward change and the ideational phase oriented toward tradition.[24] In the sensate phase, there is comparatively little agreement on values within the culture and greater pressure toward change than in the ideational phase, where transcendental values predominate and the culture seems oriented toward the past rather than the future.

One need not accept Sorokin's theory in its entirety to observe that Western musical history seems to bear out the tension between change and tradition and the tendency for society as a whole, and musicians in particular, to move from one orientation to the other over time. Contrast, for example, the persistent musical tradition throughout the Middle Ages, illustrated in the longevity of Boethius' *De institutione musica* (The Principles of Music), with the rapid and pervasive changes in the musical world during the last three centuries.[25]

Applying Sorokin's phases to the analysis of spheres of musical validity is theoretically interesting. Assume that a society moves between a traditional and a change orientation, or vice versa. It follows that as spheres of musical validity form an integral part of the cultural fabric they would likewise be influenced by, and in turn influence, these wider cultural movements. At a time of pervasively traditional orientation, we would expect less heterogeneity and a greater clarity in the range, order, and values ascribed to spheres of musical validity than at a time of change orientation, where greater disagreement about values obtains—an expectation that seems to be born out in the contrasting medieval and contemporary musical worlds. And if societies and spheres of musical validity are in process of moving (sometimes imperceptibly and at other times rapidly) from one orientation to the other, my sense of musical history is that if there is an Aristotelian "golden mean," they always overshoot it.

Traditional Accounts of the Evolution of Spheres of Validity

How do spheres of musical validity evolve? Of the traditional explanations offered, one of the most pervasive, especially among Western, classically trained musicians, even if not explicitly articulated, is what I call the "evolutionary model of musical rationalization." Its proponents hold that all music has evolved through a process of progressive rationalization toward its epitome—Western classical music.[26] The discovery of notation constitutes its crowning achievement, and "no other culture, such as the Chinese or Indian, has developed any comparably effective musical notation over the centuries."[27]

This view has been discredited in at least three ways. First, the validity of the Darwinian notion of natural evolution from which it draws has been challenged by scientists who have argued that it is simplistic and takes insufficient account of catastrophic interventions and chance phenomena in which the strongest and fittest do not necessarily survive.[28] As Attali notes, the evidence of musical history suggests that musical development has not been in a "linear fashion" from "primitive" to "classical" and then to "modern," but has been "caught up in the complexity and circularity of the movements of history."[29]

Second, some philosophers have pointed to the problematic nature of musical greatness on which the notion of musical rationalization rests. Sparshott, for example, suggests that judgments of greatness are extremely relative and meaningless outside particular musical and social contexts and also that the more prevalent concern within musical traditions is one of rightness, or whether the rules are satisfied that govern music making in a particular set of circumstances. Greatness is often conflated with importance or the esteem with which music is held in society. Rather than having to do with objective, universalistic, and intrinsic qualities, judgments of the greatness of musical events may amount to our conviction "that no being such as our selves could ever break through to the level at which such achievements are possible."[30] At very least, this argument suggests the need for extreme caution in evaluating musical quality, especially across musical traditions.

Third, ethnomusicological and anthropological evidence suggests that other musics have complexities that rival and even exceed Western classical music when judged on their own terms. Taking into account aspects of form and function, musical rationalization is therefore difficult to prove. The harmonic structure of Indian classical traditions, for example, may seem comparatively simple to Western classical musicians, although the melodic and rhythmic structure of Western classical music may appear comparatively simple to their Indian counterparts. Judgments of complexity are a matter of point of view. Since antiquity, some musics have been cultivated as classical traditions to a high level of complexity and others have remained comparatively simple and highly accessible to their publics. The distinction Plato and Aristotle made between music cultivated for its own sake (and played and sung mainly by an elite group of professionals) and that most people (mainly amateurs) sing and play has persisted in complex societies throughout recorded history. Even in comparatively simple musical traditions, judging by, among other things, the array and sophistication of their musical instruments people have developed some specialized musical functions.[31]

Another explanation is provided by what I call the "environmental model." In this view, stemming especially from anthropology, music is what it is because of environment. Steven Feld's study of the interrelationship between the physical environment, mythology, and music making of the Kaluli people of New Guinea provides an example of how this works.[32] The physical environment provides sound sources and instrumental materials, and the interrelated social environment, including myth and ritual, guides, directs, and constrains music making. Music making in turn reinforces the myth and ritual that undergirds it and reflects back on the environment, particularly on the *muni* bird (beautiful fruit dove, *Ptilinopus pulchellus*), whose position is central to Kaluli mythology and the people whose lives are interwoven with it. The model's implication—that all people living in the same environment will prefer the same music—is clearly untrue, however, especially in cultures in which multiple spheres of musical validity do exist. The spread of international mass communications and technology makes it less likely that people in isolated areas will remain untouched by the outside world and more likely that they will be attracted to other musics. This model cannot satisfactorily explain why people living in similar environments prefer different musics.

The "acculturation model" offers yet another explanation. It suggests that musical traditions are passed on through cultural contact arising out of migration and spontaneous parallel developments. The spread of musical traditions from the High Andes of the Inca empire into the surrounding lowlands, of bagpipes from Asia to parts of Western Europe, and of English brass bands throughout the British empire are cases in point. As Paul Honigsheim notes, however, "Traditional explanations for the appearance of identical phenomena in remote districts—independent parallel development, diffusion or human migration—cannot be used to adequately explain the appearance of the pentatonic scale in various geographic locations." Nor can they satisfactorily demonstrate why bagpipes gained the ascendancy in some areas, such as Scotland and Ireland, and not in others, such as England; why Eastern Slavic people prefer the minor mode and Western Slavs the major mode; and why some societies have developed classical music traditions whereas others have not.[33]

Clearly, these traditional accounts do not take us very far. They fail to account satisfactorily for the development of spheres of musical validity.

How Spheres of Musical Validity Develop

Spheres of musical validity form through five processes that collectively provide more satisfactory and comprehensive answers to the preceding questions. My list—family, religion, politics, the music profession, and commerce—is not intended to be exhaustive, but to suggest how these spheres develop.

Family

An ongoing interaction among family beliefs, mores, and traditions passes from one generation to another, from elders to youths, mainly through families and the musical ideas and practices that derive from, and feed into, these beliefs, mores, and traditions. The notion of family is an ambiguous one, referring variously to one's household, kindred (especially one's spouse, children, siblings, and parents, extending beyond to one's clan), tribe (or descendants of common ancestors), and lineage. Figuratively, it also applies to those who share common bonds of customs, livelihood, or experience and whose reality is partly articulated through music. It is illustrated in the sea shanties of British sailors, who figuratively if not literally constitute a tribe, and the spirituals of African Americans, who shared a common cultural heritage and the experience of slavery if not close kindred relationships.[34]

The interrelationships between music and family are played out differently according to whether families are organized matriarchally or patriarchally. Familial and societal value systems have impact on esthetic values and are, in turn, affected by them. Heidi Göttner-Abendroth, for example, has identified principles of a matriarchal esthetic that exemplify a radically different value system from the patriarchal esthetic that underlies much of Western and other classical music making. In her view, matriarchal art is magical and framed within the context of matriarchal mythology. Rather than the traditional author-text-dealer-agent-audience mode of communication, it constitutes "a process in which all participate collectively," "simultaneously authors and spectators." It "demands the total commitment of all participants" and is grasped holistically. Because it cannot be objectified or "subdivided into genres," the distinction between art and non-art is "redundant." It does not constitute merely a "reversal" of patriarchal values, but its "inversion" in a new and different worldview in which "the erotic is the dominant force," the "continuation of life as a cycle of re-births is its primary principle," and a "sense of continuity, motherliness and sisterly love are basic rules of the matriarchal society." Not only does this view break down the discontinuity between art and society, thereby returning art to its original unity with life, but it is also "not 'art' in the patriarchal sense of the word."[35]

Musical values reflect and reconstruct the social values that characterize family life with which they are associated. Contrast, for example, traditional Venda and classical Hindustani music making, where the former is taken to represent a matriarchal esthetic and the latter a patriarchal esthetic construed as theoretical types. Among the Venda, egalitarian relationships, inclusiveness, and cooperative endeavor are encouraged. Music making is included with the other arts, myth, and rite, classified functionally rather than formally in the context of a folk tradition, constitutes an oral practice, and is process-oriented. As Blacking observes, the chief function of Venda music making "is to involve people in shared experiences within the framework of their cultural experience." The performance of the *tshikona,* the Venda national dance, is only possible, for example, when "twenty or more men blow differently tuned pipes with a precision that depends on holding one's own part as well as blending with others, and at least four women playing different drums in polyrhythmic harmony. Furthermore, *tshikona* is not complete unless the men also perform in unison the different steps which the dance master directs from time to time." In short, Venda music evokes the notion of "the production of the maximum of available human energy in a situation that generates the highest degree of individuality in the largest possible community of individuals."[36]

By contrast, Hindustani classical music tends to be elitist, hierarchical, exclusive, formal, separated from the other arts, objectified, categorized formally in the context of a classical tradition, a notated practice, and product-oriented. Knowledge is passed down to an exclusive group of carefully selected disciples as part of a hierarchical family structure in which families of accompanists are distinguished from those of soloists (and are generally of lower social status), vocalists are distinct from instrumentalists, and knowledge is protected and kept secret by means of intrafamilial marriages.[37] Individual and small ensemble performances reflect the elitist ethic that advocates performance as something to be enjoyed by the appreciative few rather than the many uninitiated. Musicians' devotion and submission to rigorous practice schedules, by which they achieve greatness, reflect patriarchal values of self-denial, self-discipline, and work (in contrast to matriarchal values of the celebration of life, eroticism, and play).

Viewed as a social institution within a particular cultural and societal context, the family inculcates its beliefs, values, mores, and traditions in its young and ensures its survival through a life-long educational process. One of the ways in which these ideas and practices are transmitted, preserved, and reconstructed is music. Several examples illustrate. English domestic life in eighteenth-century India propagated cultural, particularly musical, chauvinism in the face of the surrounding Indian culture to which it remained oblivious and also promoted patriarchalism by gender-typing musical instruments and limiting female musical prerogatives and roles. In so doing, it reflected and reinforced the English societal values of the time.[38] Maritime Canadian folk songs "express and identify staple production," particularly that of fishing and mining, and its place in a society moving from small-commodity to industrial capitalism; provide "insight into the relations of production and consumption, of order and control"; depict a sense of regional identity and complain of the lack of parity in wealth distribution within the country; reveal such social contradictions as the "glorification of the working man, and the degrading work that men must do; in the condemnation of the bosses and merchants, and the praise of the company"; and relate to "popular culture in general."[39] The Greek women of the village of Kalohori are the "designated guardians" of vocal music. Their singing and lamenting provides both a "catharsis and commentary in response to their position in a male-dominated society."[40] Similarly, Balkan women's songs reflect their subordinate social status in a patriarchal society and various aspects of their lives, whether in birthing, marriage, the separation of the bride from her mother, or laments for the deceased, and also reinforce social customs.[41]

Returning to an earlier example, although traditional Venda and Hindustani classical music making evidence certain similarities in the way musical traditions are passed on—for example, knowledge is transmitted orally, by personal example, and word of mouth—they also reveal educational differences reflecting contrasting familial values. Among the Venda, musical ideas and practices are incidentally picked up by the entire community in an informal way through play and participation in corporate family life. By contrast, Hindustani classical music is transmitted to a select few (mainly males) in a formal manner and learned in the context of serious and pro-longed study.[42]

Religion

There is an interrelationship between musical beliefs and practices and the religious groups and institutions that both spawn and are fed by them. By "religion," I include a plethora of religious and para-religious organizations in their various mythical, mystical, ecstatic, prophetic, and other manifesta-tions.[43] Ernst Cassirer has posited that religion is a relative late-comer to civilization; before religion, myth existed as belief that was both religious and nonreligious.[44] His interpretation of religion as formalized ritual and codified belief suggests a narrower interpretation than I wish to give. I prefer to distinguish religion on the grounds that it involves the belief or sense of ultimacy, at times transcendent, that suggests various feelings of power, benevolence, dependence, mystery, intimacy, or awe in the presence of this other.[45] Put this way, religion goes beyond the established world religions of Christianity, Judaism, Buddhism, and Islam, among others, to include other communities in which a common religious experience is shared. It illus-trates diverse expressions of beliefs and rituals that also incorporate what Cassirer characterizes as the mythic precursors of religion.

Theologians and musicians alike have explored the close connection between religious belief and musical expression. [46] That music is like reli-gion does not mean that they are the same thing, however. Both are ambig-uous, demand precision, require imaginative perception, and employ a wide array of constituent elements; both are also richly nuanced, thought about, felt, and acted out in practice and yet are different symbolic systems with discrete worldviews.[47] Religion and music ask different questions. As Iris Yob puts it, "Religion wants to know . . . *what* meaning this work has for us. Art wants to know *how* this work gains whatever meaning it has for us."[48]

The relationships between religion and music are translated into practice through religious rituals, those symbolic and communal acts that express the body of understandings and beliefs underlying them. Music is often a principal, if not indispensable, element of religious ritual, religion is some-times a part of musical ritual, and the drama of religious rite is played out differently, depending on the particular religious experience that underlies it.[49] In fact, some "music" or "dance" employed in a religious setting is not regarded as music.

Within Christianity, for example, we may follow Henry Zentner in contrasting traditional Catholic and Protestant (particularly Calvinist) belief systems construed as theoretical types.[50] Catholicism holds to the importance of other-worldly rewards in heaven. Wealth here and now is relatively unimportant. Poverty is the lot of humankind. A galaxy of saints and angels joins Mary and Jesus to help the soul attain paradise. There is always the comfort of purgatory; even if one isn't quite good enough to attain heaven as a result of one's present life-long labors, prayers for the dead and offerings for one's soul might enable one to attain heaven at last. Only a relative few are priests or intermediaries between God and the rest of humanity, and few are counted among the "religious," a special group who by virtue of their dedication is closer to God. External aspects of place and time of worship are of utmost importance in creating opportunities and means whereby believers mystically experience the mystery, power, and presence of God. Architecture, music, art, and drama are essential elements in creating this sense of sacred time and place.

By contrast, classical Protestantism, although not denying the heavenly reward, emphasizes the work ethic and importance of obtaining this-worldly rewards. Time is of the essence. There is only one chance in which to demonstrate one's fitness for paradise. At the end of one's life there is only heaven or hell and no prayers for the dead on one's behalf. The galaxy of heavenly helpers is much smaller than in Catholicism, and one can do nothing to secure one's salvation except believe in Jesus and live in accordance with that belief. Members of the congregation are equal before God. All are priests and may approach God directly. Personal religious experience is of greater importance than the physical place and time in which one worships; architecture, music, art, and drama are viewed in more realistic and functional terms as utilitarian elements in the religious ritual rather than esthetic objects that enrich mystical experience.

These distinctions are reflected in the respective liturgies, particularly their musical elements. In traditional Catholicism, the cathedral is clearly divided into spaces symbolizing a hierarchical ordering between the celebrants of the mass in the choir and chancel and the worshipers (on whose behalf the service is conducted) in the nave. This spatial division contributes to a musical separation between choir, communicant, and congregation. The arts combine as integral elements within the religious liturgy to enhance its sensuous impact and thereby complement its spiritual effect. The mass is, in fact, a musical drama. Music plays an important role, with major musical parts taken by celebrant and choir and the minor musical roles in responses and hymns by the congregation. This allows greater scope for musical complexity on the part of celebrant and choir, who may be trained musicians, whereas the greater body of the congregation need not receive extensive musical education.

By contrast, traditional Protestantism insists on less division and formality in the allocation of space. The preacher stands in the midst of the congregation in a community of equals before God. Austerity rather than sensuosity is the hallmark of architecture, art, music, and drama. The congregation participates in most of the music, including hymns, chorales, and limited liturgical responses, and music plays a supportive rather than central role in the liturgy whose centerpiece is the sermon often preached from an elevated pulpit, symbolizing Protestantism's emphasis on the primacy of the word of God.

Like the family, religion educates its members in a life-long process through participating in the rituals that express its corporate beliefs, attending schools under its auspices, sponsoring that of which it approves, and censoring that of which it disapproves. Music constitutes a means through which it accomplishes its educational purposes and ensures its survival as an institution. Among the examples that might be cited, cloistered women in the Middle Ages received musical as well as theological and other instruction in addition to participating in the Office. These activities inculcated and strengthened their individual and corporate identity as a community of religious women and perpetuated the traditions of separating men and women and discriminating against women in church life.[51] Music was closely associated with the Great Awakening movements of the eighteenth and nineteenth centuries in the United States. Theological ideas spawned hymns and hymn singing, which in turn reinforced spiritual revivalism.[52] In a tradition that has continued for hundreds of years, the Church of England trained boys as cathedral choristers in its choir schools, thereby sustaining its rituals, theology, and institutional continuity.[53] And participating in Ga *kpele* rituals in Ghana inculcates and reinforces cult members' personal and corporate understandings of their religious beliefs and practices and expresses and preserves their cult identity.[54]

The particular way in which a church educates its members musically depends on the particular underlying theological beliefs exemplified in musical aspects of religious rituals. To return to the example of traditional Catholicism and Protestantism, the liturgy within Catholicism presupposed the existence of a small, elite corps of trained musical professionals and a large congregation that functioned successfully within a largely oral musical tradition. The former group required extensive musical training in schools such as the *schola cantorum,* and the latter group needed only to be regularly present at religious services. Within Protestantism, however, the congregation played a more important musical role. Mere attendance at church was no longer enough to guarantee full participation in musical and religious rituals. The entire congregation needed to be educated musically. Thus, widespread dissatisfaction during the seventeenth and eighteenth centuries with the technique of "lining out" the Psalms (in which the presentor, followed by the congregation, intoned each line of the Psalm) created impetus for sight-singing training for entire congregations.[55] Protestant pastors such as Martin Luther, John Amos Comenius, Cotton Mather, and John Curwen proclaimed the need for musical training for their congregations and were in the forefront of mass musical education movements, and music teachers worked alongside them to develop sight-singing methods and improve the quality of church music.[56]

Politics

There is a dynamic interrelationship between political beliefs, mores, and traditions and musical ideas and practices that flow from and feed into them. By politics, I refer to that having to do with the public and the state. The state has been defined variously throughout history, although several commonalities emerge. For Aristotle, the state was a "community" established with a view to "the highest good," that is to say, "a body of citizens sufficing for the purposes of life." Although it comes into existence because of the "bare needs of life," it continues to exist "for the sake of a good life." One of its principal functions is determining and administering justice that provides a basis whereby order can be maintained and the good life established.[57] As Ernest Barker puts it, "The human good, in the form in which it is provided by the state, is the energy of individual moral wills acting for their own appropriate objects in a regular system of organized co-operation."[58]

In his search for the public, Dewey suggested that the results of collective action are often unexpected and have ramifications beyond those people who are immediately concerned.[59] These unanticipated and indirect consequences of actions necessitate a political organization of officials and agencies to protect the interests of those affected by them. They form the public, which is organized in ways that regulate corporate actions of individuals and groups. Insofar as this association constitutes a political organization or something like a government, the public constitutes a political state. A state has several functions or marks: It is temporally and geographically localized, it is organized such that the actions of its members are confined within specified limits, it tends to be concerned "with modes of behavior which are old and hence well established, ingrained," and "children and other dependents (such as the insane, the permanently helpless) are peculiarly its wards."[60] Although states as we know them today in terms of their "structures" are comparatively modern institutions, "analogous functions" have been performed since antiquity.[61]

More recently, Heslep has described the normal understanding of the state as "a formal society with territorial inclusiveness, with a supreme and independent government, and with the intention of providing security for its members and a way to settle their disputes and conflicts." A state is, among other things, a society made up of "rational agents" bound together by ideals and normative rules, having moral rights and duties that oblige it to act in certain ways and constrain it to act within prescribed limits.[62]

Changes in political structure can bring about changes in musical theory and practice. This is shown, for example, in the way in which totalitarian states such as the German Third Reich and Soviet Russia influenced musical experience and performance and the ways in which composers responded to political events around them, as did Beethoven to the climactic events surrounding the French Revolution and the rise and fall of Napoleon Bonaparte.[63] Conversely, changes in musical theory and practice can foreshadow political changes. Plato recognized this when he concurred with the musician Damon that "when modes of music change, the fundamental laws of the State always change with them."[64] Music accomplishes this, argues Attali, because it "explores, much faster than material reality can, the entire range of possibilities within a given code. It makes audible the new world that will gradually become visible, that will impose itself and regulate the order of things." He also suggests that "the political organization of the twentieth century is rooted in the political thought of the nineteenth, the latter is almost entirely present in embryonic form in the music of the eighteenth century."[65]

Whatever one thinks of these particular arguments and explanations, they illustrate the historically pervasive notion that musical practice and political life are inextricable. Maybe this is because music has fundamentally to do with the exercise of power, be it political, religious, economic, or otherwise. This may be a discomforting notion for many musicians; nevertheless, Attali suggests three "successive orders," "zones," "stages," or "strategic uses" of music for purposes of power. As a simulacrum of ritual murder or sacrifice, music has "ritual power" in that it makes people forget their fear of violence; when it enters economic exchange as a part of enactment and spectacle, music has "representative power" in that it makes people believe in order and harmony in the world; when it is reproduced and repeated, music has "bureaucratic power" in that it silences those who oppose it. "Beyond repetition lies freedom" that heralds new social relations as music revolts against normality and becomes composition.[66]

It is not necessary to accept all of Attali's theory to agree that music may serve different types of political powers and purposes. If it does, and the evidence seems conclusive, states use at least four principal means to exercise these powers musically: censorship, sponsorship, legislation, and education. Through censorship, states act to prevent that which is considered subversive from being heard. They constitute a filtering mechanism whereby only that music within the range of what they consider to be acceptable is composed, performed, and listened to. Totalitarian states such as Nazi Germany, Soviet Russia, and the People's Republic of China (particularly during the cultural revolution) have exemplified strict musical censorship of one sort or another.[67] Democracies such as Australia, Britain, Canada, and the United States have likewise censored music by controlling and monitoring broadcasting and institutionalizing "the silence of others" in order to assure the continuation of their powers.[68]

States use sponsorship to encourage and support musical beliefs and practices of which they approve. Musical patronage—notably the maintenance of composers, singers, and instrumentalists in European courts from the fifteenth through the nineteenth centuries—has served important political purposes and is part of a tradition that stretches back to antiquity.[69] States have also established patriotic occasions for the singing of national anthems and patriotic songs, such as the hymns of the French Revolution and Nazi Germany's political rallies (in which mass singing constituted an important means of social control).[70] Countries such as the United States, Britain, Canada, Sweden, Tanzania, and Cuba have provided grants-in-aid to musicians and subsidized and sponsored musical events. And the transition from state subsidization of music to its privatization in Chile had a profound impact on the musical life of that country.[71]

Through legislation, states enact policies that directly and indirectly control various aspects of musical life and establish the institutional frameworks within which these policies will be carried out. Although the specifics of policies vary from one country to another, they share the common thread of channeling musical composition and performance in certain directions and within prescribed limits. U.S. legislation on the arts, for example, has touched on such issues as censorship of material that offends public sensibility, sponsorship through such organizations as the National Endowment for the Arts, and the regulation of education, broadcasting, copyright, recording rights, and royalties. Legislation also has impact on musical life by causing cultural contact or acculturation through forced or voluntary migration. The importation of African slaves into North America, for example, resulted in a fusion of aspects of African and European musical traditions in jazz, gospel, and rock.[72] Canadian immigration and multicultural policies also introduced and preserved East Indian, Arabian, Caribbean, Doukhobor, and Mennonite musical traditions in various parts of Canada.[73]

Through education, states seek to inculcate musical beliefs and practices that will be consistent with their methods and ends and ensure their survival. The most important educational strategy is that of musical schooling under the auspices of the state. State officials and their representatives shape the musical knowledge considered to be legitimate, enact policies that ensure these objectives will be met, and devise methods for musical instruction consistent with their enunciated objectives. One of the principal concerns, especially in small countries, has been the survival of indigenous musical cultures, and school curricula in such small countries as Hungary, Brazil, Jamaica, and Tanzania have reflected these concerns.[74] Beyond the schools, states have used the mass media as means of life-long education of citizens. Since its inception, for example, the British Broadcasting Company has been an educational agency of the government and has constituted the model on which former British colonies and other countries have based their own government-sponsored broadcasting operations.[75] Music educators such as Percy Scholes, Carl Orff, and Gunild Keetman have developed approaches to music education through radio broadcasts.[76]

Conversely, the political power that musicians exercise through music making subverts or preserves the status quo. Wolfgang Mozart's attack on aristocratic privilege in *Le nozze di Figaro* (Marriage of Figaro); Giuseppi Verdi's calls for Italian independence in *Nabucco, I Lombardi, Ernani,* and *Macbeth* and his political commentaries in *Simon Boccanegra, Otello,* and *La forza del destino;* Bedřich Smetana's critique of Czech politics in *Dalibor* and *Libuše;* and Nicolay Rimsky-Korsakov's thinly disguised commentary on Russian political events in *Zolotoy petushok* (The Golden Cockerel) are cases in point. Even such instrumental works as Smetana's *Má vlast* provide "a composite picture of what is meant by a nation's cultural heritage," "a ringing answer to the overlords who, in order to oppress and enslave a people, will try to wipe out from their minds the memories of their own heroic and independent past."[77] On the other hand, some composers align themselves in the service of the state. Heitor Villa-Lobos and Hans Werner Henze, for example, sought to exemplify in their compositions the principles that underlay their respective states and that they adopted as their own. In his *Bachianas Brasileiras,* Villa-Lobos combined folk music and Western classical music evocative of Brazilian nationalism, and in his Second Piano Concerto and Sinfonia Number 6 Henze united soloists and orchestral players in an egalitarian interplay that he believed consistent with Marxist thought.[78]

Like the family and church, the state educates its members directly in schools and indirectly through participation in the life of the state. Likewise, the particular beliefs, values, and mores that a state holds have impact on the nature of the educational process. Contrast, for example, schooling in a democratic capitalistic state, such as the United States, with that in a totalitarian socialist state, such as Hungary, during the forty years after World War II. Underlying the U.S. democratic ideal is tension among the claims of individuality and collectivity, freedom and discipline, which develops people to their fullest potential while also reconciling them to social control. Dewey and Herbert Read agreed that the method or process of democracy and its underlying tensions must be expressed within schooling.[79] It is not surprising, therefore, that the U.S. school system is decentralized and marked by methodological and curricular eclecticism as various forces express these tensions differently.[80] By contrast, communist Hungary faced a different set of tensions as it prepared its citizens for the pervasive and different claims of social control while it enhanced their individuality. Its school system modeled a more directive and highly structured approach that was centralized and exemplified comparative methodological and curricular unity.[81]

Two school music methods that represent these contrasting positions are the Keetman-Orff *Schulwerk* and the Kodály choral method. The Keetman-Orff method is ideally suited to democratic thinking. It employs exemplars rather than directives in a loosely structured manner that can be readily adapted by teacher and students; it invokes improvisation and performance as the principal means whereby learning takes place; it is immediately accessible to all the participants in that it does not necessitate prior musical literacy or skill acquisition; it involves a multifaceted approach to musical learning through speech, song, dance, and instrumental performance (on pitched and nonpitched instruments in a variety of timbres); and it is process-oriented in that its major focus is on the experience of music making rather than the achievement of a particular end. By contrast, the Kodály method conforms nicely to totalitarian thinking. It employs a strictly regimented, carefully sequenced set of tasks to be followed by teacher and student; it relies on a capella choral singing; it emphasizes delayed gratification in which musical skills are mastered systematically in the hope of eventual musical literacy; and it is product-oriented in its focus on prescribed ends.

The Kodály and Keetman-Orff approaches have advantages and limitations. In order to remedy the limitations of the one approach, American music educators incorporated elements of the other as a counterbalance. The result created an additional and different set of problems concerning the reconciliation of tensions between the two approaches. In the absence of a national centralized educational system, various approaches emerged to the means and ends of music education. Meanwhile, Hungarian music education continued until the end of the communist regime, with a more or less unified approach centered on the Kodály system and largely untroubled by the eclectic challenges faced in U.S. music education.

The Music Profession

An ongoing dynamic interrelationship exists between the beliefs, mores, and traditions of the music profession and musical ideas and practices. The word *profession* is somewhat problematic and ambiguous. Its dictionary meanings connote an avowal, a body of knowledge, and a group of people organized around that body of knowledge. Considered as a social institution, a profession can be characterized in terms of at least the following symptoms.[82] In order to be part of a profession, an individual must master a body of received wisdom sufficient enough to preclude most people from having ready access to it; considerable training is mandated to acquire the required knowledge by such means as apprenticeship, internship, and other forms of formal and informal instruction; organizations and mechanisms exist for admitting people to membership and guaranteeing that their conduct falls within certain acceptable limits or according to given norms; specialized language is employed that is intelligible only to initiated members of the profession or those otherwise granted access to its knowledge; the body of knowledge forming the basis of the profession includes an important component of craft or skills that are practiced artfully; and at least some members of society value the wisdom possessed.[83] There is also an avowal or commitment to pursuing and practicing the received wisdom as a way of life and direct contact with clients who attempt to direct the professional's work and remove patronage if they are dissatisfied.[84]

In the West, musicians have associated together since antiquity, notably in ancient Egypt, Greece, and Rome, in medieval guilds, and in modern musicians' unions and professional associations.[85] As music became a commercial product, especially when it became a spectacle on the scale of the past two centuries, musicians found it necessary to organize in order to promote their economic well-being, mutually protect their livelihoods, and prevent exploitation by others.[86] The flowering of the Western classical tradition and the rise of the modern European concert patronized mainly by the middle class prompted a change in musicians' status from servants of the family, church, and state to independent artists. And a variety of organizations such as the modern orchestra, choir, opera house, and conservatory included the framework of the music profession.[87]

Musicians are influenced by the musical ideas and practices characteristic of the traditions in which they work. They also reconstruct these traditions and create new ones, especially through their writings on, and activities in, music education.[88] Nicholas Wolterstorff captures this tension when he observes that the artist working in the context of a particular musical "practice" or activity of music making in which one must be inducted "allows social realities to *guide* her composition" such that "*invention itself is channeled.*"[89] Thus, Beethoven, heir to Enlightenment thinking and the classical ideals exemplified in the music of Haydn and Mozart, demanded greater freedom and subjective expression and more massive and potentially dramatic instrumental forces than earlier musicians had imagined. And Ives, heir to New England Transcendentalism and working within the religious and musical context of early-twentieth-century America, mandated a new musical technique and sonority. Each can be seen as a protector of the past and a herald of the future.

A similar tension is evident historically between musical institutions and musical beliefs and practices. Like the family, church, and state, the music profession, through its various institutions that served as its "gatekeepers," sponsored particular musicians and musical styles, censored ideas and practices, and educated the public; it was also partly shaped by social and musical events outside its control.[90]

Historically, professional and amateur musicians coexisted, sometimes amicably and other times unhappily (especially where professional livelihoods were threatened).[91] Although differences between professionals and amateurs are sometimes unclear in practice, the distinction is theoretically useful. Stebbins suggests, by way of clarification, that the evolution of what were once play activities into "modern amateurism" came about partly because of the pervasiveness of excellent professional performances. Modern amateurs, he posits, constitute a part of a professional-amateur-public system of "functionally interdependent relationships." They share characteristics of professionals in that they "serve publics," they are related organizationally and monetarily to professionals who often train and perform with them, they have intellectual relationships with professionals, and they understand, possibly better than the "run-of-the-mill" members of society, what constitutes an appropriate performance. They restrain professionals "from overemphasizing technique and other superficialities in lieu of a meaningful performance or product," insist "everywhere on the retention of good taste," and furnish "professionals with the stimulus to give the public the best they can."[92] If there is a distinction to be made, he concludes, it is to differentiate amateurs from professionals, principally in terms of the direction of their occupational commitment, their self-conception (they think of themselves as amateurs and sometimes experience frustration at the high performance demands of them), and their position within the professional-amateur-public system.[93] Allowing that distinctions between amateurs and professionals are sometimes fuzzy in practice, Stebbins's multifaceted approach constitutes a useful point of departure in differentiating them as theoretical types.

These typical differences, seen more or less in practice, translate into corresponding contrasts in music education. In the *Republic,* Plato mandated a simpler musical training for the citizen's general education than that required of the professional performer. This classical duality between one sort of musical education for the professional (who must earn a livelihood in music) and another for the amateur (whose commitment and livelihood is gained elsewhere and whose musical training must perforce be more limited) is historically resilient. Despite the fact that famous amateurs such as Henry VIII, Elizabeth I, and Frederick the Great were, by all accounts, outstanding musicians, published instrumental treatises and compositions demonstrate that mass musical education, especially from the Renaissance on, was considered to be qualitatively different from that of the preparation of professional musicians.

Professional musicians must acquire practical skills for a future livelihood and maximize educational opportunities in order to gain certain musical competencies, irrespective of how appealing the process of acquiring them is. The necessity of gaining a livelihood from music motivates them to forgo present pleasure, undergo intensive and rigorous training, and dedicate a great deal of time to the process of becoming a musician. Such musical virtuosity is often acquired in the context of individual or small-group instruction that is more or less elitist. Historically, like Johann Quantz, students received formal instruction through apprenticeship. Like Felix Mendelssohn, they received individual instruction from expert musicians (musicians are fond of tracing their musical lineages); in conservatories, where they followed a formal, practically oriented program of performance, history, theory, and composition in the tradition of the seventeenth- and eighteenth-century Venetian conservatories; and in universities, which historically, especially throughout the Middle Ages and the Renaissance, had an academic rather than practical orientation.[94] Students also received informal instruction and learned incidentally through participating in music making.

By contrast, amateurs enjoy music making for hedonistic reasons. Without present or anticipated future rewards, they can more easily opt out of the music-making process. Not only is time more limited because of other claims outside music, but they are also less willing than professionals to forgo present pleasure in the music-making process and undertake rigorous training in some aspect of music unless there are compelling reasons to do so. For them, the acquisition of virtuosic performance skills may constitute a lower priority than general musical training. Because they greatly outnumber professionals, a universalistic approach in the context of mass musical instruction is called for that necessitates accessible, popular music composed specifically for amateur study and performance. Amateurs historically receive formal instruction through individual music lessons, as did Susanna Perwich, a Puritan woman whom Scholes chronicles, in classes such as those conducted in the New England singing schools or in amateur ensembles such as various British choral societies.[95] They also benefit from informal instruction and incidental learning through participating in the process of group music making evident, for example, among the Balinese musicians and dramatists whom Margaret Mead observed and in jazz jam sessions.[96]

Commerce

A dynamic interaction exists between commercial or business beliefs, mores, and traditions and musical ideas and practices. By "commerce," I refer principally to those businesses that are distinguished by their motivation to sell goods and services in the expectation of a profit within such considerations as the public good.[97] This concept is somewhat ambiguous in at least two respects. First, commerce capitalizes on scientific discoveries and technological inventions that may lie outside its purview. Although they are interrelated practically, science and technology are conceptually distinct from commerce. Nevertheless, seeing that inventions have impact on music making principally through the activities of commercial enterprise, and that both are linked intimately, I include them here, allowing that the edges of commerce, where commerce blends into science and technology, are fuzzy.

Second, societal institutions such as the family, church, state, and music profession engage in commercial enterprise motivated by other than strictly economic considerations. Besides direct involvement in business activities, these institutions affect the market by controlling the production and distribution of goods and services through censorship and patronage, among other means. Because it is virtually impossible to separate the actions of businesses from these other organizations in the marketplace, I shall subsume all such activities within commerce. This conception may err in the direction of being too inclusive rather than exclusive, but it allows me to focus on the role of commerce, broadly construed, in the formation of spheres of musical validity.

The interrelationship of commerce and music making is supported by various sorts of evidence. In their study of popular music from 1948 to 1973, for example, Peterson and Berger found a relationship between market concentration and musical homogeneity or diversity. Periods of market concentration corresponded to musical homogeneity, and periods of competition corresponded to musical diversity lagging behind competition. Relatively long periods of increasing competition were followed by short bursts of competition and diversity in which market structural changes preceded musical changes.[98] Rosanne Martorella has demonstrated a relationship between American opera house income and repertoire diversity. When income is insecure, insufficient, and opera companies rely primarily on box office receipts, companies retreat to standard, popular operas and less innovative programming.[99] And in an analysis of the international music industry Laurence Shore suggests that public musical taste is shaped not so much by record companies directly controlling the music product as by their exclusion of alternatives.[100]

There a connection between economic prosperity and the degree to which the arts flourish, and Raynor has shown how international trade has played an important role in musical diffusion. Musical ideas and practices flowed along trade routes; peripatetic musicians, especially from the Renaissance on when they were freed from church employ, contributed to the progressive internationalization of musical styles; and prominent banking families such as the Fuggers promoted musical innovations.[101] Commercially used printing inventions further enhanced the spread of music and developed an international market for composers.[102]

The rise of a European, commercially oriented, middle class changed musical life and taste. The middle class demanded amateur ensemble and solo music for home use, and its demand was met with printed salon music and private musical instruction that eventually culminated in the widespread growth of amateur music making in the eighteenth and nineteenth centuries.[103] Music teachers such as Muzio Clementi published and peddled printed music that emphasized style over substance and accessibility over complexity, and audiences patronized performances by superstars, virtuosic and dramatic spectacles, thereby changing the face of operatic and concert performances.[104] A mass musical culture emerged throughout the late eighteenth and nineteenth centuries, the product of such entrepreneurial breakthroughs as the establishment of an international network of retailing outlets and burgeoning musical publishing, instrument manufacture, and concert management industries among other commercial developments. And the mass musical events that typified concerts of the late nineteenth century became increasingly impersonal and exploitative; they symbolized and "celebrated the emerging urban industrial civilization with a grand thronging together in public places."[105]

Wiora has posited that as music became widely available to people of all social classes, a bourgeois musical culture replaced a patrician musical culture.[106] Musical tastes became splintered into various musical subcultures, with esoteric musics at one extreme and popular musics at the other.[107] Technology had profound impact on the nature of music and became embedded in it.[108] Musical institutions assumed control of all aspects of musical life.[109] The specialization of musical functions and the elimination of people by technology resulted in their playing a less human role in music making. At the same time, as Etzkorn has pointed out, technology offered the potential for greater personal involvement in music.[110] Whatever one thinks of these changes, there can be no doubt that they dramatically affected musical life and taste.

The musical industrialization of the nineteenth century ushered in an era of global expansion of Western music in which capitalistic ideas, especially the specialization of labor, predominated. The period was marked by technological inventions, especially those in mass communications, and culminated during the latter part of the twentieth century in an international music industry dominated by an oligopoly of transnational companies (primarily American, European, and Japanese interests) concentrated in the Western industrialized world. These companies, in turn, were constituent elements of mass-communications companies that controlled all aspects of musical life—composition, performance, publishing, recording, marketing, and, ultimately, listening—through an international network of subsidiaries, licensing arrangements, franchises, and other business connections. They achieved their dominance through such strategies as concentration, integration, and diversification.[111]

The impact of Western music on the rest of the world through the activities of commercial enterprises had important consequences for musical ideas and practices internationally. Wiora describes the globalization of music, that is, the rise of a monolithic global music culture strongly influenced by Western music but potentially yielding an "extraordinarily rich and multiform" musical life. This variety of musical expression could arise, Deanne Robinson, Elizabeth Buck, Marlene Cuthbert, and their colleagues point out, by virtue of the concomitant indigenization of music, the growing desire among musicians to maintain a "local cultural identity" in the face of an internationally pervasive musical culture.[112] Others, such as Roger Wallis and Krister Malm, envisage several possibilities, transculturalism among them, in which each culture draws from and contributes to an overarching global culture.[113] Still others, Bruno Nettl, for example, see the response of musics outside the West as primarily a process of modernization in which other musics adapt to Western musical influences without losing their essential features. The result, he argues, was an unprecedented variety of world musics, although somewhat altered by the impact of Western ideas and practices.[114]

Whichever of these views eventually turns out to be correct, many governments found the situation to be extremely problematic. They have enacted policies designed to preserve their respective cultural heritages in the face of what they see as a pervasive Western influence, particularly that of American popular culture, that threatened to swallow up indigenous musical cultures.

Music making also has a significant impact upon commercial enterprise. A noteworthy twentieth-century example is provided in the response of the popular music industry to the development of rock and roll. During the late 1950s major companies were surprised by the resilience of rock music, which they had first assumed to be a fad. They had either to adapt to these new circumstances or lose their market share. Businesses were also forced to change the way they treated rock stars because of their growing contribution to company profits and their financial acumen and insistence on making artistic decisions about their recordings. The financial success of rock music contributed to the growth of the recording industry and also generated a plethora of associated industries: public relations, artist management, concert production, and video production.[115]

Commerce often seems reactive rather than proactive in regard to musical taste—it responds to what it thinks people want. Peterson observes that rather than seeking to shape musical taste according to its own esthetic or artistic criteria, it systematically excludes musical possibilities. It makes these determinations based principally on quantitative and fiscal rather than esthetic or artistic criteria, so much so that the "most potent censor of art works is not police, patron, or Pope, but profit."[116]

As Wallis and Malm note, however, the degree to which music businesses are motivated by fiscal considerations differs along a commercial/noncommercial scale.[117] At each extreme are music businesses distinguished on the basis of their commercial or noncommercial (or musical) orientation. At the commercial extreme, shareholders and management make the major decisions, the organization is structured hierarchically, tasks tend to be highly specialized, and artists occupy a relatively low place in the hierarchy. A desire to maximize profits drives the organization, music products that do not sell quickly and in sufficient quantities to justify the costs incurred in their production and distribution are not easily tolerated, and shareholders receive profits. Marketing aims to create demand, by manipulative or exploitative means if necessary, and each product is distributed to as many people as possible.

By contrast, at the musical extreme, business decisions tend to be made collectively and involve artists in a more egalitarian organizational structure where tasks tend to be less specialized. Decisions are governed principally by artistic concerns and expressed consumer needs, there is greater tolerance for products that sell more slowly over a longer period, and profits are used to promote new products or for nonprofit purposes. The company is more interested in making a lot of music and minimizing losses or breaking even than in maximizing profits. Marketing is focused on consumer information, and each product is distributed to specific consumer groups who share the same values and interests as the company.

In industrialized countries, companies have operated historically in the context of economic environments that have restricted, controlled, or encouraged capitalistic enterprise. Contrast, for example, a planned economy in which market forces are restricted and welfare economic considerations are paramount with a capitalist economy in which market forces operate principally in response to demand and supply of goods and services. In a centrally planned economy, the state dictates the range of acceptable music, terms of musical production, and distribution and profit-taking; establishes rules and regulations for business operation; and issues authoritative esthetic and artistic criteria based on supporting, sustaining, or reflecting values that the state espouses. By contrast, in the absence of authoritative esthetic and artistic values, profits assume the principal criteria for musical enterprise, and a "welfare of critics, reviewers, moralists, and 'taste-makers'" shape what is sold. Musicians and businesses are free to explore various means of musical production, distribution, and profit-taking, often within bureaucratic organizations that assume control of most musical decision making.[118]

Within these market constraints, both types of firms educate their publics in different ways. In the industrialized world, both use mass media, exclude musical alternatives, and are motivated by the desire to make a profit. Among their differences, music education in commercially oriented companies tends to be exploitative and manipulative, constitutes a form of propaganda, appeals physically and emotionally rather than intellectually, satisfies transitory impulses rather than establishes long-term educational goals, searches for novel sounds and sights to attract attention, silences rather than encourages active music making, relies on informal learning through hearing and rehearing music counted by media promoters to be worthy of attention, and embraces quantitative and hedonistic values in adjudicating music. By contrast, music education in musically oriented companies explores shared values, invites people to participate in the learning process, appeals intellectually rather than physically and emotionally, embraces tradition as well as change and the discovery of new techniques, encourages active music making, uses formal as well as informal instruction, and adopts esthetic and artistic values appropriate to music making of whatever genre it promotes.

MTV represents a commercially oriented business approach to music education. As Serge Denisoff explains, the company's objective was to provide music targeted at a specific age group—the "rock culture" or the "television babies who grew up on TV and rock 'n' roll." The program format was specifically geared to "grab" the audience through its "aura of calculated 'laidbackness.'" In his attempt to put together a "format with the proper mood-evoking programming," one senior executive and architect of MTV stated, "The strongest appeal you can make is emotional. If you can get their emotions going, forget their logic, you've got them. . . . MTV fits in with all of this because music deals with mood, not continuity or plot." Seen as a societal threat by parents, politicians, school teachers, religious leaders, and feminists, accusations of MTV's violence, racism, and sexism had "little if any effect." The response was rather a defensive posture: "Those who criticize the violence and sexual suggestion in the videos are committing the first cardinal sin of rock and roll appreciation. They are taking things much too seriously."[119]

The British firm of Novello and Company, on the other hand, exemplifies a musically oriented business approach. Michael Hurd has described its contribution to the outburst of creative music making, especially by British amateurs during the nineteenth century, and its fostering of new as well as old music by publishing cheap, widely distributed music in a variety of classical and popular styles.[120] Novello's attempt to improve public musical taste contrasts sharply with MTV's marketing strategy of pandering to public demand irrespective of its musical taste. The firm attempts to educate public musical taste rather than capitulate to its uninformed elements, even at the risk of lower demand for its goods and services and smaller profits.[121]

Implications

Exploring some of the ways in which music is interrelated with society, particularly how social expectations of music arise, how music feeds these expectations, and what impact various societal institutions have on musical ideas and practices and are, in turn, impacted by them, reveals five processes: familiy, religion, politics, the music profession, and commerce. Although they are conceptually distinct, the processes interact; the institutions to which they contribute and from which they draw are themselves interrelated. This approach provides a means of exploring grounds for the diversity of musical beliefs and practices throughout the world.

These ideas have important implications for music education. Recognizing that spheres of musical validity exist, and understanding the reasons why they come into being and are maintained, provides a basis whereby music educators can more intelligently and comprehensively plan their work. Seeing music and education as part of a complex network of cultural and social beliefs and practices suggests that music educators must understand these contexts and integrate their work within them. If music is a part of life rather than apart from it, it cannot be studied in isolation. Rather, it must be seen as an important aspect of general culture.

Spheres of musical validity suggest that music education is not all of a piece but is a collage of beliefs and practices. Its role in the formation and maintenance of spheres of musical validity associated with different societal institutions—each with distinctive values, norms, beliefs, and expectations—implies disparate ways in which music teaching and learning are properly carried on. Understanding this variety suggests that there may be multifarious ways in which music education can be conducted with integrity. The search for a single, universally acceptable theory and practice of musical instruction may provide limited understanding. Instead, a comprehensive picture includes many different phenomena that count as music education, institutions with which it is associated, and processes by which it is characterized.

It is also necessary to adjudicate the various spheres of musical validity. All do not have equal or universal claim on our attention or support for a host of moral, ethical, political, religious, musical, and practical reasons. Some spheres conflict with others. Some are difficult to reconcile with others. Notwithstanding these difficulties, it is incumbent upon music educators to weigh these claims and devise strategies that meet them directly.

If music education is to be truly effective, some way must be found for these processes and their affiliated institutions to work more or less in tandem, even if in tension, rather than at odds. In the process, the musical and educational beliefs and practices on which music education is based, and to which it contributes, may require change. Herein lies an important challenge for music educators and their public.

Essaying some answers to the question, What is music? has raised an array of tantalizing theoretical and practical problems for music educators. Aside from the issues relating to which musics to teach, the questions relating to how to reconcile the various sorts of music education carried on by the family, church, state, music profession, and business—among other societal institutions with an interest in transmitting musical beliefs and practices from one generation to the next—are enormously problematical. Finding solutions to these questions and enabling various institutions to work in consort with others will be challenging, especially because music educators have thought in terms of more limited objectives in the past and many are committed to, or comfortable with, the status quo. They will need the understandings and skills to work in a wide array of contexts—as church musicians, professional performers and composers, private studio teachers, music business people, recording engineers, and designers of computer software. Individually, they will need to learn to better forge links among the various institutions interested in music education. Corporately, the profession will need to further strengthen its ties with other cultural agencies so as to design strategies that focus the efforts of various institutions on comprehensive interinstitutional approaches to music education. Work on these projects has already begun, but this analysis provides further grounds for music educators to expand their thinking systematically beyond the needs of elementary and secondary schools to other possibilities.

Music educators have historically been concerned with the realization that their work is ultimately a multigenerational enterprise. The musical education of school students is a natural place to begin. Parents, grandparents, and extended family members are important influences on the young, however, and music educators need to be concerned with the family environment in which children are growing up. How to provide assistance for parents in raising their children musically and culturally must be a primary concern of music educators for whom musical enculturation is an objective. Some music educators, notably Suzuki, have already developed plans for directly involving families in musical education. Others are involved in community music schools of one sort or another. The broader conceptual view of music education suggested here, however, justifies exploring other ways of planning systematically for familial music education.

Since its introduction into state-supported schools, music education has maintained at least informal ties with church music. Music educators often serve as church musicians along with their school teaching or academic positions. Within parochial schools, sacred music remains an important, distinctive feature of general education. And many churches employ teachers to direct their amateur and professional performing organizations—choirs, bands, chamber music ensembles, and the like. Yet the vision of religious music education suggests going further to integrate these musical activities more systematically into a comprehensive scheme of musical education. This means, for example, working directly with churches to improve the quality of musical instruction and seeing these activities as a vital part of music education as surely as music instruction in the schools. There are other possibilities besides.

Including the activities of professional musicians as a branch of music education also has important practical implications for music educators. The various instrumental pedagogies—voice, brass, string, woodwind, and percussion—and their respective specialties must surely benefit from such an expanded view. So can theory and composition pedagogy, jazz pedagogy, and conducting pedagogy. These areas are the legitimate province of music educators as much as of the various specialists who practice them. The perspectives of music education can help provide a broader and better basis for instruction in such areas. For too long these pedagogies have been excessively narrow in their focus. Regrettably, they have also been marginalized within the music education profession. It is time to reclaim them as legitimate music education specialties and work closely with their practitioners. Theoretical and empirical research has already focused on various aspects of advanced instrumental, vocal, and theoretical music instruction, and redrawing the conceptual map of music education would validate this ongoing work.

Commercial interests play an important role in contemporary music education. Including these interests invites developing strategies that directly meet the economic and financial preoccupations of our time. Viewing business as an essential area of music education means rethinking how to prepare people with the business acumen and musical and educational skills necessary to improve the quality of commercially available pedagogical materials. In particular, music educators need expertise in the technological skills related to computer hardware and software development, sound synthesizers, music publication, and instrument manufacture, allowing them to be designers as well as consumers of such materials. Indeed, business people who are also committed music educators can potentially improve musical instruction and enhance the quality of musical experience for composers, performers, and listeners.

The multiple perspectives on music education arising out of the various spheres of musical validity and their associated developmental processes again suggest the prospect of dialectics between one sphere and another, one developmental process and another, and one societal institution and another. Tensions arise within each process from the differing perspectives of various societal institutions, social groups, and individuals. And determining the particular mix of musics and the respective roles of various institutions in the music educational enterprise raises a host of theoretical and practical challenges that require the brightest minds and most concerted efforts to solve. These issues cannot be reduced to simple or easy solutions. Rather, music educators, individually and collectively, must tackle them anew as each generation faces the challenges of its distinctive time and place.

Having addressed the questions of what is education and what is music, I shall move on to discuss several dialectics that music educators face and that arise out of the nature of music and education and between philosophy and practice. In taking this tack, I am following the thread that has already emerged in the foregoing discussions of music and education. This dialectical approach offers a synthesis of a particular sort. Rather than attempting to bring conflicting ideas or tendencies into reconciliation, unity, or harmony, music educators may sometimes need to be content with disturbance, disunity, and dissonance. Things in dialectic do not always mesh tidily, simply, or easily. Nor necessarily ought they. The resultant complexity, murkiness, and fuzziness of these dialectical relationships, however, greatly complicate the task of music educators.

A Dialectical View of
Music Education

Throughout history, music educators have faced challenges that are, in some respects, remarkably similar and in others unique to a particular time and place. In our time, we confront dramatic worldwide changes. Rapidly advancing information technology has facilitated global communication on a scale and speed unparalleled historically. Political, religious, economic, and social upheavals in remote parts of the world can be known about instantaneously. North American and European culture can be transmitted easily and cheaply worldwide, foreign influences cannot easily be controlled by local and state authorities, and cultures, previously sustained by such boundaries as geographic, political, religious, and linguistic differences, are threatened by others.

The effect of these cultural changes is to raise compelling questions for music education internationally—questions that have yet to be addressed fully within the community of music educators and that offer a rich basis on which to revise the profession. That music educators have yet to examine these questions systematically is not surprising given that twentieth-century philosophical thinking in music and music education has principally come out of the West, especially the United States, the United Kingdom, and Germany, and has grappled mainly with issues germane to these countries and the Western classical music tradition. Comparatively recently, however, under the prompting of the International Society for Music Education, the profession has begun to take a more global view and tackle issues raised in our time.[1]

What are these questions? In raising some of them, I shall suggest a set of paired concepts in which one is dialectically related to the other. Each pair constitutes a dilemma for music educators. They may be loosely categorized into two groups, musical and educational issues, although I prefer to think of them collectively. Together they comprise a broad view of music education and are interrelated, and the whole also seems greater than the sum of its parts.

The Dialectics

Musical Form and Context

Susanne Langer has described music as having articulate form, one piece in turn made up of parts integrated with other parts in such a way that the whole appears to have meaning and significance apart from its individual elements.[2] Rather than making a comparison with a clock in which one can identify components that together go to make up the mechanism, she prefers metaphors of a waterfall or a stream, in which the whole has life, vitality, and dynamism. In pointing to music's formal structure as understood by composer, performer, and listener, and as the musician's central interest, Langer does not discount music's cultural context. Her study of Cassirer's work made her well aware of the plethora of world musics and their varied place in society—from the rituals in preindustrial societies in which the arts, myth, and ritual were united to the fragmentation of the arts and other ways of knowing in the contemporary West. Nevertheless, she does not doubt that it was classical Western music that should remain the focus of musical education, construed broadly. As a cellist, she composed and performed classical music. She followed in the tradition of Kant, Arthur Schopenhauer, Eduard Hanslick, and others, believing that the answers to musical meaning lay within the study of the music itself. Studying music, one could find expressed the same feeling—construed variously as physical sensation, cognitive emotions, and emotive cognitions defying propositional discourse—that exemplifies human nature.[3]

This view has prevailed in the West since at least the Enlightenment; one can trace its roots to antiquity and other classical traditions. The Greeks' elaborate, mathematically based theory of music carried forward to the Christian era, exemplified in Boethius' *De institutione musica* and thence, in succeeding centuries, underpinning the development of the Western classical music tradition. The rise of what Kivy calls "music alone"—instrumental music designed for contemplation and organized in such forms as the sonata and the fugue—continued the Western interest in the formal structure of music.[4] Likewise, in the East, Indian classical music based on theoretical ideas, partly paralleling notions of the West but nevertheless with a different flavor, developed in an alternative tradition grounded in an appreciation of formal structure. To be sure, context was important in the East as it was in the West. But a musician's principal interest was in developing and understanding the structure itself and faithfully representing it. Whether it be a sonata or a *dhrupad* (an old Hindustani compositional style), musicians were—and still are—compelled and impelled by considerations of musical form that are primary, at least at the moment of performance and hearing.

In failing to take up sufficiently the question of musical context as an issue bearing importantly on musical meaning, Langer is not alone. Others, such as Leonard Meyer, acknowledge the importance of culturally designated musical expectations outside the Western classical tradition and then analyze Western classical music as the music they know.[5] It remains to anthropologists, ethnomusicologists, and sociologists such as Merriam, Walter Kaufmann, Blacking, Nettl, and Shepherd to point out that context is vitally important in determining musical meaning and should not be relegated as ancillary to formal characteristics.[6] Understanding context is a key to grasping music's formal characteristics.

These writers have shown that Western classical music constitutes a slice of the world's musical traditions, and although music might be a more or less universal element of human culture, its language is by no means universal. Western classical music does not necessarily constitute the all-important key to understanding other musical traditions as previously assumed. Rather, they argue, musical traditions must be understood in their own terms, according to their particular underlying beliefs and practices. These traditions cannot necessarily or readily be generalized. And new means have to be found in order to analyze them. The vocabulary used in the analysis of Western classical music, particularly common practice, is inadequate in describing the entire corpus of the Western classical tradition, let alone other musical traditions.

These insights raise two problems for music educators: First, Are they to emphasize musical context or form or some combination of both? Second, Which of the many musical traditions are they now to teach? With respect to the first question, they might be tempted to embrace both alternatives, thinking that they can do justice to contextual and formal aspects of music.

But the issue is more problematic than at first glance. As a practical matter, musicians trained in the Western classical tradition have been and still are more comfortable with formal than contextual analysis, primarily because of the nature of their musical training. Contextual issues have also proved much more difficult to analyze than at first thought. Ethnomusicologists have encountered serious problems developing theoretical systems on which they could agree, for example, and that would enable analysis and comparison of particular musical traditions. Witness the still formative theoretical state of ethnomusicology.

The idea that social context governs musical experience turned out to be a simplistic view. It became clear that certain aspects of musical experience might be universal, and the idea of contextualizing music, although important, need not be all-important. Notions such as the "collective unconscious" suggest possible explanations for these commonly experienced attributes of music and the apparent ability of music to transcend a particular culture from which it emerges and to which it properly belongs. Whether it be in Bali or Kenya, Brazil or Australia, Fiji or the Ukraine, people sometimes experience music similarly, and they employ sounds in meaningful ways, both vocally and instrumentally. Listeners unschooled in, or unfamiliar with, a particular music can appreciate a performance of it, at least to a limited degree. These ideas and observations suggest that although both form and context provide keys to understanding music, one is not necessarily more important than the other.

Viewing the Western classical tradition (along with its concomitant folk traditions) as a slice of the world's music within the context of spheres of musical validity focuses attention on many musics, each with its own formal and contextual attributes and worthy of study. In recent decades, North American music educators, among others, have sought to include various traditions of world music in their curricula. The intent might be the noble one of valuing each musical tradition for its own sake, but the sheer enormity of the task and the limitations of teacher training may lead to such pitfalls as tokenism or exoticism of the kind that provides inadequate sampling of world musics or a superficial treatment of them. Given their lack of understanding of world musics and the immensity of the potential repertoire, teachers naturally worry about which of all these traditions their curriculum can encompass and how they should approach the task. What if students become conversant in other musical traditions and neglect their own?[7] Reconciling the claims of musical form and context complicates musical education, and resolving these issues is not easy.

Notwithstanding these difficulties, that music is both formal and contextual and composed of substance and manner that are dialectically related, music education should be broadly based. Every piece of music, of whatever tradition, should be approached from the perspective of its place in the social fabric and with a view to discovering its inherently musical properties. One without the other constitutes an unbalanced and insufficient position. How to balance these attributes becomes an important practical consideration.

Great and Little Musical Traditions

In analyzing culture, researchers at the University of Chicago during the 1950s and 1960s developed the notion of great and little cultural traditions.[8] Great traditions are generally those that have developed an international following and are revered as highly developed cultural products, complex, notated with an extensive written tradition, ethically elitist, and practiced mainly by professional artists. Little traditions, by contrast, are often localized, constrained by social class and ethnicity, somewhat simpler in construction, not necessarily revered as great works of art, mainly oral traditions, ethically universalistic within certain constraints, and practiced mainly by amateurs. These theoretical types constitute a means for separating classical musical traditions (e.g., European, Indian, and Chinese) from folk musical traditions without necessarily imposing normative value judgments upon them. They also provide a way of envisaging two opposite emphases in music education: literacy (principally associated with mature great traditions) and orality (mainly revealed in little traditions).[9] In music theory and practice these symptoms are more or less evidenced in various world musics, although with important caveats: Mediated musics—those popularized through the media—exemplified in contemporary jazz, rock, and country have become international musics while still retaining some of the qualities and popular appeal evocative of folk music, and the distinction between written and oral musical traditions is fuzzier than the theoretical distinction between great and little cultural traditions implies.

In the West, the gulf between the great and little musical traditions has been widened by a tendency to elevate a canon of classical musical works above the level of the ordinary and set this canon in stone.[10] In the process, music educators may forget that the relationship between great and little musical traditions has always been, and continues to be, symbiotic. One draws from and influences the other and reflects the dominant power groups of the time. Among those music educators who have recognized this link, Kodály maintains that knowing folk music is basic to the development of musical education. He argues persuasively that no music is too good to be studied by the young and that only the most exemplary music should be incorporated into the curriculum, whether it be folk or classical.[11]

Kodály distinguishes between traditional folk music—music making by local people in the countryside—and popular music (what I have referred to as mediated music, that emanating from cities and towns). In his view, popular music contributes to bad taste in the arts, which he characterizes as "a veritable sickness of the soul."[12] I am less inclined than Kodály to banish popular or mediated music from the curriculum summarily. For one thing, the impact of technology, especially in recent years, has blurred distinctions between what Kodály would have thought of as popular or mediated music and indigenous folk music. Composers in each of the classical, folk, and popular or mediated streams continue to draw from the others as they have always done, making it difficult to argue for purity in each case.

Kodály might also be faulted for inappropriately applying Western classical esthetic criteria to other musics and looking at all musics through the eyes and ears of a Western classical composer. If we grant some degree of universalism in musical experience, however, he is not entirely wrong in so doing. Whatever its faults, the Western classical tradition has become a truly international musical language, a great musical tradition understood by people all over the world. Among its most devoted adherents are Eastern musicians, and its composers, performers, and audiences represent people from all social classes, languages, and ethnic backgrounds.

I am not persuaded by the argument that classical traditions are necessarily elitist and tied inextricably to the bourgeoisie whereas folk and popular traditions are necessarily universalistic and inevitably proletarian. Marxist attempts to equate music with social class and class struggles are inevitably overdrawn and tend to emphasize the differences among, rather than shared qualities between, various musical traditions. Neither classical nor folk music has a corner on greatness, goodness, or rightness. And the line between great and little musical traditions is fuzzy as one merges into the other.

Attempts to democratize music by emphasizing popular musical culture at the expense of classical traditions are misguided. They fail to recognize every musician's desire for immortality through her or his composition and performance—to be remembered as having achieved greatness, whether for hedonistic or other reasons; to attain the normally impossible or difficult; and to create something significant, even unique if possible, whether cooperatively or individually. That classical musical traditions have developed in various societies constitutes a monument to human aspirations for excellence, transcendence, and immortality. Human genius has never been plentiful, and it is unfortunate if it is devalued by suggesting that exhibitions of quite ordinary and sometimes inferior talent are great and equally worthy of study just because they are popular. To do so is to elevate mediocrity as the ideal and even to discourage students from pursuing musical excellence. If the classical music tradition does not have a corner on greatness, we may well find musical gems among the folk and popular idioms and, conversely, quite ordinary examples of music in the classical tradition. Democratic ideals imply equality of opportunity to create rather than creative output; to confuse the two is to make a significant mistake. A teacher's search for musical repertoire necessarily includes both great and little musical traditions and seeking out that which is special, distinctive, meaningful, and within the powers of students to realize successfully.

If great and little musical traditions have a place within the curriculum, reconciling their respective claims, at least practically speaking, remains a question. The concept of balance between great and little musical traditions is fraught with difficulty. Deciding which ought to be emphasized, the direction in which one should move (whether from the little to the great tradition or vice versa or from one to another little or great tradition), and how to solve the problems of curriculum construction so as to avoid superficiality and tokenism are just some of the problems to be settled. Integrating rather than simply accommodating different musical traditions is a far more complex problem than simply following one musical tradition. Avoiding the pitfall Kodály notes, that of learning several musical languages poorly rather than at least mastering one's own, necessitates careful consideration and practical planning on the part of music education policymakers.

Transmission and Transformation

Music educators likewise find themselves caught between the claims of the past and those of the present and future. Historically, the great body of music education has been devoted to transmitting a musical heritage from one generation to the next, exemplified most clearly in the master-disciple tradition of northern India and individual or small-group instrumental and vocal instruction in the context of the Western conservatory or private studio. Whether it be in a disciple's studious imitation of the teacher's sitar playing or the pianist's absorption of technique from an artist teacher, the focus is on transmitting wisdom and values from the past in as pure a form as possible. Consequently, the various Indian *gharanas* (familial and stylistic schools of performance) and the Western schools of piano performance share attributes of faithfulness to various musical beliefs, practices, principles, and techniques.

More recently, educators have called for transformation in society and cultural life and nothing short of a revolution in the educational process. Among them, Paulo Freire and Maxine Greene have argued that much has been wrong with the past: The revolutionary ideals of liberty, fraternity, and equality espoused in the eighteenth century have yet to be truly realized.[13] In place of freedom, there is oppression; in place of fraternity, there is divisiveness; and in place of equality, there is inequality. Barriers that have historically separated people—conditions of age, gender, color, language, ethnicity, sexual identity, religion, wealth, and social class, among a host of other differences—still remain. Educators have a responsibility, these writers have posited, to redress society's evils and act as agents in its transformation and regeneration. Simply transmitting values from the past without questioning their veracity, relevance, practicality, or vision is failing to do the work of an educator in the fullest sense of the word. As such, it is, by default, oppressive and miseducative.

Likewise, feminist writers such as Göttner-Abendroth have criticized what they see as a pervasively patriarchal esthetic undergirding classical artistic traditions. They would like to replace this esthetic with a matriarchal one that, among other things, eschews objectifying the artistic object and replaces it with a focus on the interaction between self and artistic object and an emphasis on the artistic process; negates the pervasive cognitive emphasis in understanding the artistic object, celebrating instead the bodily and emotive aspects of artistic and esthetic response; denies the hierarchical and linear relationship between creator and observer or between composer, performer, and listener, emphasizing rather the idea of egalitarian and communitarian enterprise in the artistic process; and repudiates the idea of art as an elitist enterprise apart from the populace, insisting instead that art is an inclusive process that comes from the people and is performed with them.

For music educators, these ideas mean transmitting beliefs and practices, revisioning the music profession and, ultimately, impacting present and future society. The Tanglewood Symposium in 1967 called for them to participate in the reshaping of society.[14] David McAllester went so far as to argue that "the entire Music Establishment is the perpetrator as well as the victim of a hoax" and that "the controlling middle class in the United States does not *see* the lower classes and the poor among them" and is "profoundly unwilling to face the invisible culture"—those in the inner cities, the poor, and the mentally disadvantaged. To enable "true musical communication with the great masses of our population," it would be necessary to affirm that "while we continue to develop and make available, to all who are interested, the great musics of the middle class and aristocracy, we must also learn the language of the great musical arts which we have labeled 'base' because they are popular." By so doing, McAllester hopes that music educators can "reduce the class barriers in our schools and our concert halls," give to music "a new vitality at all levels, and provide a united voice that can speak, without sham, of our democratic ideals."[15] Such a revolution would mean recasting notions of tradition to include oral as well as literate musical traditions, vernacular as well as classical music, and reshaping the face of America, an avowedly political ideal.[16]

A generation later, problems of overpopulation, poverty, illiteracy, economic and social dislocation, hunger, political upheaval, religious animosity, and inhumanity remain. Still, I cannot agree with McAllester that Western classical musicians have been caught up in a hoax. "Hoax" is too strong and insidious a description. Rather, my reading of history suggests that classical musicians and their patrons cultivated a rich musical tradition that they genuinely believed would contribute to the betterment of humankind. Its wide appeal cannot be attributed entirely or mainly to the supposed machinations of a particular social class. Nor can I agree with feminists who argue that a matriarchal esthetic will necessarily improve the situation. Instead, it may simply replace one form of oppression with another. Esthetic characterizations of this sort inevitably turn out to be theoretical types, offering theoretical perspectives on musical belief and practice and yet, practically speaking, remaining problematic. This is because every theoretical categorization that is drawn includes some things and perspectives and excludes others; therefore, no theoretical system can be devised that is all-inclusive.

Attributing particular musics to certain classes and allowing only a certain range of esthetic and artistic experiences can be patronizing, even oppressive. To escape being marginalized in society and lacking political, social, and economic empowerment, all need the understandings and skills to move beyond their limitations and constraints and function with others. People must be empowered to change society. The classical music tradition need not remain outside people's grasp because they lack the skills to understand it, or the folk or popular music they count their own be ridiculed or belittled in the process of achieving that understanding. Education ultimately prepares people for an unclear future, and music teachers, as in any field of study, desire to enrich their students' capacities for transforming the present into a hopefully better and brighter future. Freire's term *conscientização* (conscientization, or "learning to perceive social, political, and economic contradictions and to take action against the oppressive elements of reality") is particularly interesting here because it combines reflection, a sense of personal and corporate conscience, with the willingness and ability to act to transform the present.[17]

North American music education research and practice has begun to focus on student interests and preferences without concomitantly emphasizing the principal role of these interests and preferences as springboards for, rather than the central preoccupations and ends of, music instruction. Transforming music and society ought not serve as an excuse for pandering to students' present musical interests and capitulating to their immediate desires and preferences. Rather, it should also take into account what they can or might become in the future with appropriate and sufficient preparation. Schiller observed that the artist who gives the public what it does not like, yet what he or she believes it should have, becomes an irritant to society.[18] Regrettably, yet necessarily, the same is true of teachers who provide students with things they may not presently want in the hope that these things will be better for them and for society at large.

Many barriers to understanding a classical tradition remain, not the least of which are the complexity of its formal structure, its literate and technical requirements. Barriers also stand in the way of understanding other musical traditions, including different scale systems, foreign timbres and rhythms, and contextual assumptions. Music teachers wishing to provide broad perspectives on, and experience of, music must necessarily focus on great and little traditions that are otherwise elusive. Scholes observes that removing these obstacles to understanding constitutes an important element in enabling people to grasp the Western classical tradition.[19] His metaphor of removing roadblocks to musical understanding might be enriched by that of building bridges between one musical tradition and another.

Practical problems also remain. Music educators are conflicted about how to transform society and still hold on to what they perceive to be the musical wisdom of the past. They wish to give a musical voice to the presently disenfranchised while also enabling them to know other musical traditions. Various musical organizations have attempted to do this, notably the Glasgow Orpheus Choir during the first half of the twentieth century and the more recent Boys Choir of Harlem. Both choirs achieved an international reputation and perform a wide repertoire of folk through classical music throughout the world, their respective members striving individually and collectively for excellence. Notwithstanding such achievements, many music teachers grapple with problems of how to balance past and present and be sensitive to the need for transformation in some respects and the importance of transmission in others. They wrestle with questions of balance between the two and also with deciding the particular directions in which transmission and transformation should be directed.

Continuity and Interaction

One of the principal problems of designing music curricula relates to its scope and sequence—how broad the curriculum should be and how music educational experiences should be ordered. Dewey explained that two qualities or dimensions—continuity and interaction—are vital to constructing an educational process enabling personal and corporate growth.[20] Both form what he called the situation—the present educational circumstance in which teacher and student find themselves. "Continuity" refers to the attribute of one thing leading logically and inexorably to the next; "interaction" denotes the contemporaneous interrelationship between this thing and other things. In Dewey's view, each experience, composed of what we might think of as vertical and horizontal dimensions, leaves a trail of effects that creates the potentiality for growth or atrophy. Such effects can never completely be erased. The present situation, therefore, is invested with urgency and importance for teacher and student alike.[21]

Curriculum, at least in the view of such writers as Philip Phenix, Greene, and Michael Apple, is the process whereby students experience subject matter from not just the teacher's perspective but vitally and from personal interaction with it.[22] Curriculum is not just a set of topics that the teacher sets out and reviews during the instructional process, even if its objectives do follow from a study of the students as Ralph Tyler suggests; it is a dialogue between teacher and student—and student and student—that is invested with meaning for all concerned.[23] Students' interests, abilities, and ideas are enlisted in what becomes a life-changing process charged with intrinsic meaning rather than characterized by extrinsic rewards and products.

Dewey's concept of the experiential situation assumes relevance as a framework in which to design a curriculum that possesses these characteristics. Rather than being controlled by textbooks or methods, teachers assume the role of professionals instead of technicians in designing for a specific situation the sorts of experiences that they judge to be continuous (that draw directly from students' previous experiences) and interactive (that relate or are perceived by students as relating to other situations, both musical and otherwise). It is a vision of curriculum that becomes a means whereby teacher and student are each valued contributors to a dynamic process.

In weighing the demands of interaction and continuity, music teachers face several practical dilemmas, among them deciding whether or not to emphasize local, national, or international musical traditions and—if all are important—how to balance the emphases on these respective traditions. There are several alternative approaches to reconciling the claims of various musical traditions, whether they be locally, nationally, or internationally based. Music education might focus only on folk musical traditions from a local area or country or only on those classical traditions with an international scope. Or it might focus on an international view of music from which it is then possible for students to work back to a national and local view of music, a national view of music and then work outward in two directions—one international and the other local, a local view of music and then work outward to a national and subsequently international view of music, or local, national, and international views of music more or less simultaneously.

Focusing only on local and national traditions might pass the test of continuity in respect of students' past and present experiences, but it fails to provide sufficient scope for musical study. Conversely, focusing only on international musical traditions might fail the test of continuity even though it provides a conservationist approach to world musics, particularly its classical traditions. We might likewise eliminate the alternative of starting with an international view and then working back to a local view because doing so fails the test of continuity in respect of the past and present experiences of students except insofar as mediated musics count as international traditions. For the same reason, we might eliminate the alternative of starting with a national view and working toward local and international understandings, especially if a state is multicultural. Given that few countries are culturally homogenous, I am inclined to believe that this alternative may prove to be problematical. The last two strategies seem to offer approaches that exemplify, at least theoretically, continuity and breadth of musical experiences. Given the present state of musical exchange internationally, it seems likely that students might work concurrently at all these levels within the context of a gradually expanding musical horizon.[24]

The problem of interaction is a vexed one because it necessitates contextualizing the curriculum, understanding music in terms of the various contexts in which it is made and experienced and also within the framework of a student's entire program of education, whether formal or informal. The test of curricular scope, therefore, must address these contextual issues if it is to meet Dewey's additional requirement of the interactive aspects of experience. Applying this stringent principle may help music education policymakers plan how to enable students to move from an understanding of their particular musics to those of their country and the world beyond.

It is imperative that the movement from a child's home through the various levels of schooling—elementary, secondary, and tertiary, and on to adult life—be thought of as one continuous process. Unfortunately, it seems that discontinuities occur between children's home education and the point at which they begin to attend school, between each of the levels of schooling, between the time students complete their schooling and begin adult life, and between the musical experiences and values embraced by schools, churches, families, businesses, and governments, among other institutions involved in music education. Some music educators, notably Suzuki, have devoted considerable attention to early childhood musical education, but in general most curricular development—in the West at least—has focused on the music education of school-aged children and youth (and that discontinuously) and on elementary, middle, or early secondary, high or later secondary, and college or university music education. Continuing or lifelong music education, and geriatric music education, especially in the case of aging populations in the West, also require emphasis, as does music education in the context of other institutions besides schools. If the needs and interests of adults vary, as the work of Erik Erikson suggests, music educators will need to broaden their focus to study how people come to know music throughout a seamless, life-long process.[25]

Making and Receiving

In describing the nature of artistic experience, Dewey made a distinction that still has relevance. He suggested that experiencing the arts involves personal action and responsiveness. By action, he thought of individuals engaged vitally in artistic expression, much as a composer or performer is involved in making music, or "musicking." Such action, however, is also taking place as observers or listeners study a painting or listen to a symphony. Both are imaginatively constructing and reconstructing visual or aural images and making meaning of what they see or hear in terms that are their own and not necessarily those of the creator in each case. Just as wine is "expressed" from grapes, Dewey reasoned, so individuals encounter difficulties to be surmounted in making and understanding a picture or a symphony. Impulse encounters obstacles to be overcome; the artistic experience makes demands on individuals that must be met and surmounted if expression is to occur.

By contrast, Dewey suggested, artistic experience has a passive dimension in the sense that people allow the artistic event to happen to them, both as part and consequence of the artistic process. In so doing, they demonstrate such qualities as receptivity, sensitivity, openness, and even vulnerability to the work of art, whether it be the painting or the symphony. It happens to them just as much as it happens through them. They are active agents of the artistic process and also recipients of it.

Although we need not accept Dewey's particular view of artistic expression in entirety, his insight that the experience of art involves both active and passive dimensions—what I call making and receiving—is of the greatest importance for music educators. That he envisaged these two aspects holistically rather than dualistically raises the question of how they are to be reconciled and balanced within the music curriculum.

Dewey saw difficulties inherent in the English words *esthetic* and *artistic*. "Esthetic" applied, in the philosophical literature at least, to the experiences of observers or listeners; "artistic" used to describe the experience of the composer/performer or "creator" of the art work.[26] He was at pains to draw these two words together, showing that distinguishing them bifurcates the experience of art and artificially and even wrongly separates elements that are and should be perceived as a unit. Nor did he denote the active element of the artistic experience as artistic and the passive element as esthetic. Quite the contrary. Dewey emphasized the maker's role as sensitive to that which she or he is in the midst of creating and the observer's and listener's active role in imaging the work of art and thus bringing the artistic process to fruition.

Recent thought in music education has focused on artistic aspects of music making rather than the esthetic experience that has prevailed for several decades in North American music education.[27] The distinction highlights semantic difficulties arising from the use of such descriptors for music education as esthetic and artistic education and suggests qualitative differences in the music education process, especially relating to matters of musical form and context. Music educators may fall into the trap of making the equation to which Dewey refers, of ascribing the esthetic to the listener's experience and the artistic to the performer's and composer's, thereby equating artistic with the active and esthetic with the passive receptive elements of musical experience. In so doing, they may bifurcate the experience of music and fail to see it in broader terms.

The music education profession is in need of a broad perspective that accepts, embraces, and even celebrates both the making and the receiving of music, recognizing that all the actors in the process—composer, performer, and listener—are equally participatory in, and recipient of, the musical experience, albeit in possibly different ways. No actor or activity is necessarily at the center of the music educational process; making and receiving are essential elements of the musical experience.

Such a view creates a dilemma for music education policymakers, who must reconcile the claims of making and receiving in the context of an holistic musical experience. How should students make and receive music? How might the balance between various forms of making and those of receiving be struck? Technological innovations, particularly in the present century, have created new ways of making and receiving. In particular, mass media has enabled the recording and replaying of music on a scale unprecedented in the past, putting a premium on musical listening and introducing new ways of hearing music in individually experienced and electronically reproduced performances as opposed to those experienced corporately. These developments present enormous potentials and problems for music educators because they revise the musical experience as well as its underlying belief systems. For example, the development of computer-generated sound and digital sampling, among a host of other innovations, offers to reconstruct the making or doing of music. Computing has changed the face of musical composition and altered performance radically. Instead of painstakingly practicing a fugue, for instance, it is possible to program it on a computer and replay it effortlessly. Even the notion of live sound is now problematical, such is the impact of electronic media and other means of sound manipulation.

These changes in compositional, performance, and listening possibilities call into question traditional belief systems by making them irrelevant and raising new musical and other issues as well. Not only do they suggest normative questions about particular roles of making and receiving and the balance between the two, but they also challenge the necessity of preserving the past in the context of a pervasive emphasis on the present and future. Technology looks forward. Its emphasis is upon what is now and, more important, what can be in the future. It is impatient with the past. It presses for transformation rather than transmission, for developing new ways of experiencing music. As a result, whether in the Americas, Asia, Europe, or Australia and Oceania, music educators must consider weighing the claims of making and receiving in a technologically oriented world that promises new ways of music making but at the same time threatens to silence it and offers new ways of composing, performing, and listening to music yet emphasizes passive musical consumption.

Music educators can respond to these challenges by coopting technology within their programs while balancing the claims of individual expression and those of technological innovation. From antiquity, music arising from the body—singing—has remained distinctive from instrumental and technological means of sound production. Singing constitutes a means of music making that can stand entirely apart from technology. If students are to understand that technology cannot and should not supplant the individual human being's expression, they must experience music making in non-technological ways, suggesting that a substantial part of musical experience should be gained through singing.

In the United States, singing seems to have declined, notwithstanding its importance and despite the efforts of some music educators. In its place, instrumental music education seems to have gained the ascendancy. Perhaps this is because of the power of technology and people's preoccupation with it, along with other social and cultural factors. If instrumental music forms a major means of musical expression, however, and students are preoccupied with acquiring technical mastery over their instruments rather than participating in singing, they may fail to experience a uniquely human musical expression possible without the aid or intervention of any technical or instrumental means. Learning to sing provides vital understanding of what Howard calls the "art-craft"—the "arty craft" or the "crafty art"—of music that complements and enriches other technologically and instrumentally gained insights.[28]

Discovering means of music making and receiving that are both dependant on and independent of instrumental and technological means complicates the problem of reconciling music making and receiving. It necessitates thinking through issues of how composition, performance, and listening should be balanced and integrated within the curriculum, and how instrumental and choral music should be reconciled. Various curricular models have been suggested by such writers as John Paynter, Keith Swanwick, and June Boyce-Tillman, but further theoretical work is needed, especially in the context of the various dialectics that have been discussed.[29] Still, balancing and integrating vocal and instrumental programs in the context of making and receiving music provide for a broader and richer music educational program than would otherwise be the case, one that is especially relevant to a technologically oriented world.

Understanding and Pleasure

Kant made an important distinction between two aspects of esthetic experience: understanding, in which observers or listeners grasp the meaning of the art object, and pleasure, the sensory and emotional response that the work of art elicits. Understanding, he believed, involves an imaginative grasp of, or mental play with, the art object and may elicit a pleasurable experience. Pleasure, on the other hand, is merely an emotional response to the sensory stimulus that the work of art constitutes. The object of attending to works of art, Kant argued, is that of exercising judgment—the keystone in his trilogy of types of intellection complemented by pure and applied reason—constituted within the framework of broad teleological principles developed in the latter part of his *Critique of Judgement.* Following Kant, many educators have construed understanding as central to the esthetic experience and, by extension, the music curriculum.

Kant's distinction was carried forward in Schiller's distinction between work and play. Among other things, Schiller construed work as that which involves reason, invokes discipline, denies present gratification in the hope of future reward, and represents serious effort that is not necessarily pleasurable. By contrast, play invokes imaginative thought and activity, celebrates freedom, and embraces present gratification without necessary regard for future reward. Schiller argued that work and play, understanding and pleasure, and reason and imagination are all involved within the esthetic experience.[30]

Dewey invoked these dialectics of understanding and pleasure and work and play in his writings on the nature of artistic and educational experiences. Art, he believed, cannot be separated from the rest of life, of which it is an integral part, and its serious intellectual contemplation ought not be divorced from a sensory and emotional enjoyment of it. Likewise, education involves both work, construed as serious effort devoted to future ends, and play, or imaginative celebration of the present.

Although the correspondence is not one-to-one, attaining understanding can be compared to work and experiencing pleasure to play. This does not deny that play may be involved in the process of coming to understand a work of art and that work may be pleasurable, but simply suggests that the emphases in each case are different. Viewed as continua, work and play seem more like understanding and pleasure, respectively.

Intellectual understanding has generally been accorded a high value within educational philosophy and practice, and sensory and emotional pleasure has been downplayed because of its acquired hedonistic and frivolous connotations. Consequently, music educators have been at pains in recent years to demonstrate that musical study is concerned principally with understanding rather than with pleasure and brings knowledge—whether of music, self, the world, or whatever may lie beyond—that is experienced privately and shared corporately. Efforts of music educators in this country and abroad to develop national standards of musical excellence and student achievement witness this preoccupation. And I do not deny its importance.

At the same time, some music educators have historically recognized the important role of pure pleasure and sensory enjoyment. They have believed that some music is created just to be enjoyed now rather than understood in the future in some deep and meaningful way and after careful deliberation. The Shoshone do not necessarily stop to analyze the musical structure of their social dances before or while they engage in them, for example; they perform them for the sheer pleasure and fun of doing so. True, these dances have meaning, intuitively and rationally grasped. Yet providing social and individual physical abandonment and hedonistic enjoyment is their primary reason for being. They constitute celebrations, and play, in much the same way as the ancient Greeks understood play. Shoshone music is judged on primarily physical rather than intellectual criteria. In the process of learning these dances, whether as singers, instrumentalists, or dancers, the Shoshone people experience the pleasure of the dance as a primary ingredient of musical instruction.[31] Likewise, in the European tradition, elementary school music teachers, particularly those in the early grades, have embraced pleasure as an important instructional principle. Activities, whether songs or musical games, are judged with reference to arousing children's pleasure as an important aspect of the music-learning process, as a means to some end and as an end in itself.[32]

During the educational process, the delight in pleasure and imaginative play in music curricula in the early grades often gives way to an emphasis on understanding and reasoned musical work in later grades. Developmental models such as those by Alfred North Whitehead, Michael Parsons, and Swanwick and Tillman are sometimes cited as a basis for this progression, notwithstanding that, as Whitehead posited, the cycles (or "rhythms") from romance through instrumentation to generalization involve dynamically changing emphases on understanding and pleasure throughout the entire educational process.[33] In view of a widespread human delight in play, it would not be surprising if student interest in musical instruction declined throughout the educational process, especially if acquiring understanding becomes preeminent and work assumes priority while pleasure diminishes and play all but disappears.

Recognizing the tension between musical understanding and pleasure and validating both—seeing both as having a contribution to make to the educational enterprise—opens a richer range of curricular possibilities than is possible in the absence of such a dialectic. It suggests embracing musical activities that celebrate the making of music now without necessary thought for future performance and selecting enjoyable experiences that provide immediate pleasure. In so doing, music teachers capitalize on students' personal interests and desires, both as an end in itself and as a means to future development. When students see that the educational process provides rewards to be experienced now as well as in the future, musical study becomes contextualized and invested with meaning and intrinsic value.

Practical issues arise in the process of striking a balance between understanding and pleasure, choosing instructional methods and repertoire, and designing music curricula. Dewey insists that teachers ought not to pander to students' present interests and pleasure, keeping in mind the claims of continuity and interaction. In celebrating pleasure as an end as well as a means, teachers are faced with selecting instructional methods, strategies, materials, and activities that can accomplish this without sacrificing understanding, and herein lies the challenge. Particularly in class instruction, the wider the range of student musical abilities, interests, and achievements, the more complicated the teacher's task. Many students receive musical instruction outside the school. The practical constraints of scheduling music classes within the school and achieving the sorts of more or less homogenous groupings possible within other academic subjects is challenging and sometimes impossible, particularly in later elementary and early secondary school grades when music is a compulsory subject of study. In later secondary schools, colleges, universities, and in subsequent adult life, instructional groups may become more self-selective according to students' interests and abilities.

Negotiating educational means and ends, processes and products, creates problems. Musical understanding lends itself to product-oriented, outcomes-specified approaches, including music achievement tests and other forms of assessment; pleasure delights in process and resists testing, being content rather with the enjoyment of the educational process itself. Product- or outcomes-oriented curricula and assessment approaches emphasize understanding and prejudice pleasure, and yet educational authorities often demand them as measures of accountability. Finding ways to promote accountability without prejudicing pleasure necessitates ensuring a wide array of assessment procedures beyond the traditional criterion-referenced and standardized tests.

Philosophy and Practice

Yet another dialectic is that between theory and practice. Joseph Schwab and Scheffler have pointed out that the worlds of philosophy and practice do not correspond exactly.[34] Philosophical principles are capable of translation in a variety of practical ways, each of which may be reconciled with the same principles, and the process of moving from philosophical assumption to practical outcome is an artful one. As Schwab puts it, the process can be described as the "arts of eclectic" in the sense that each principle holds within it the potential for a cluster of practical and interrelated applications. Seeing one application is only to view a portion of the possibilities inherent within a particular idea. Similarly, each principle is interrelated with others, and it is difficult to isolate the practical impact of one idea from that of another. Principles are theoretically contradictory or capable of conflicting applications and also sometimes seen in incomplete or distorted ways. Thus, in the classic case of the blind man and the elephant, where the man "sees" only one part of the elephant at a time, the process of translating theory to practice involves working with incomplete views.

Acknowledging this discontinuity and even tension between theory and practice, between one theory and another and one practice and another, provides some clarification. Although educators, among them musicians, have sought the high road to musical understanding, it is unlikely that such a way is possible. Rather, music educators may need to be content with admitting a variety of ways in which people come to know music. It is unlikely that any practice can ever be based on any one coherent set of assumptions—or that any one set of assumptions constitutes a philosophy or theory capable of only one set of concomitant practices. In reality, any set of grounding principles is likely to yield tensions, discontinuities, and even paradoxes. That is because translating these principles into reality is fraught with difficulties, compromises, limitations, and even hostilities. It is difficult, outside an idealized situation, to imagine how any given set of principles could be translated perfectly. We have only to witness the history of philosophical ideas in education and the problems encountered in applying them to practice.

Were educators content with the limitations of philosophy and theory as the foundation for educational practice, they would see that this limitation constitutes, paradoxically, a strength. Belief systems—whether construed as ideals, precepts, guiding principles, analytical skills, descriptive tools, or whatever—place teachers in the position of artists and craftspersons who must creatively apply such ideas to their individual situations. Rather than technicians who employ methods indiscriminately without reflecting on their appropriateness, teachers critically reflect on practical problems and apply various ideas, techniques, or skills to them. As such, the undergirding assumptions for their practices draw from, as much as contribute to, those practices.

The preoccupation with musical instruction methods, at least in the West during the past two centuries, has been counterproductive in that it has fostered the notion that there is a one-to-one correspondence between philosophical assumptions and practices. The fact that instructional methods have been worked out to a high degree of sophistication and defended as if they were dogma is oppressive to teachers. It fosters their dependance on methods and those who promote them and on passivity, timidity, meritocracy, technocratic attitudes and behaviors, and even anti-intellectualism construed as a lack of interest in and reflection about questions that underlie practice.

When teachers see that there is no one high road to music education practice and that their responsibilities lie in translating principles into practices they are empowered as artists, craftspersons, and professionals to devise methods that creatively and imaginatively suit the needs of their students. In so doing, they see that music education is like science and may be based on certain generalizable principles, even laws; like art, it is known and exhibited in many ways that are particular, subjective, and nongeneralizable. This in itself is a paradox.

Implications

A dialectical approach to music education presents questions and challenges that have to do with the relationship of musical form and context, great and little musical traditions, transmission and transformation, continuity and interaction, making and receiving, understanding and pleasure, and translating theory into practice. Rather than searching only for scientific laws that undergird a single "best practice," music education researchers should also seek ideas and practices that are appropriate for or right in certain situations. They should value description as much as scientific explanation, even if its results seem murkier, less generalizable, more complex, and even contradictory, because description can get at some things that other investigative means cannot. The demands of each situation cannot be met by a single universal philosophy or method of instruction no matter how philosophically and practically defensible it might appear to be. Rather, each music teacher must fit the right instructional approaches to a set of demands in some measure unique to a particular situation.

Such a broad view requires reshaping the music education profession. It necessitates preparing music teachers to make decisions as professionals rather than technicians, equipping them to cultivate a wide understanding of the meaning of education and the role of music as a cultural phenomenon and handle the dialectics they face in their classrooms, studios, and all the other places they teach. It means enabling music education researchers to undertake a wide range of philosophical and scientific studies and validating descriptive as well as analytical investigations. It requires rethinking the role of music education in conserving and reshaping aspects of music and education and providing a clear vision for the future. It suggests seeing the possibilities for music education inherent in the context of several institutions—the family, church, school, business, and music profession, among others—as a life-long rather than school-age pursuit. It requires courage to act in variance with institutional pressures to preserve the status quo if need be. And it demands moving beyond the uncritical acceptance of the ideas and methods of others and becoming critically and personally engaged in asking questions and finding the right instructional approaches for the particular situations educators face.

A critic might suggest that music educators are incapable of grappling with such issues. They require others to do it for them. They cannot learn to love the questions. They need to be led, given ideas, methods, and materials by others more gifted, educated, or experienced. Not so. If music teachers are apathetic and dependent on the leadership and instructional methods of others, it is because of how they have been prepared as teachers and what has been expected of them throughout their careers. Overcoming their reluctance to tackle these issues for themselves necessitates reexamining how they are trained and what opportunities exist for continued personal and professional development.

Music teachers can be professionals in every sense of the word. They can contend with these issues successfully. They can ask and address penetrating questions. They can make informed, careful decisions that meet the needs of the students with whom they work if they have the preparation and freedom to do so. Just as a chorus of singers rises to the expectations of its conductor, so educators can rise to meet the challenges of musicians, educational policymakers, and the public. The music education community must provide the kinds of preparation and incentives that will enable teachers to develop as professionals empowered to make their own decisions rather than remain as technicians who follow the directives and suggestions of others.

The various conceptions of education, spheres of musical validity, and dialectics of music education are problematical, and the questions they raise and the challenges they present are demanding. Nevertheless, together they suggest a rich basis for revising the discipline in ways called for in the present world and also, where necessary, preserving ideas and practices from the past. They also open the possibility for exploring the many ways in which people come to know music throughout the world.

Notes

Chapter 1: In Search of Music Education

1. John Dewey, *Democracy and Education: An Introduction to the Philosophy of Education* (1916; repr., New York: Free Press, 1966), 4, observed that the relationship between society and education is so intimate that "society not only continues to exist *by* transmission, *by* communication, but it may fairly be said to exist *in* transmission, *in* communication."

2. On the notions of classical, folk, and popular music, see *New Harvard Dictionary of Music,* ed. Don Randel (Cambridge: Harvard University Press, 1986), 172–73, 315–19, 646–49. Throughout, I use "Western classical music" to refer generally to music of the Western classical tradition rather than specifically to music of a particular style from the mid-eighteenth to the early nineteenth centuries.

3. Jacques Ellul, *The Technological Society,* trans. John Wilkinson (New York: Vintage, 1964); Neil Postman, *Teaching as a Conserving Activity* (New York: Dell, 1979); Alvin Toffler, *The Third Wave* (Toronto: Bantam, 1981); Fritjof Capra, *The Turning Point: Science, Society and the Rising Culture* (1982; repr., Toronto: Bantam, 1983).

4. As Rosemary Radford Ruether notes, *"Gaia* is the word for the Greek Earth Goddess, and it is also a term adopted by a group of planetary biologists, such as James Lovelock and Lynn Margulis, to refer to their thesis that the entire planet is a living system, behaving as a unified organism." See *Gaia and God: An Ecofeminist Theology of Earth Healing* (San Francisco: Harper, 1992), 4. See also James Lovelock, *Gaia: A New Look at Life on Earth* (Oxford: Oxford University Press, 1979); James Lovelock, *The Ages of Gaia: A Biography of Our Living Earth* (New York: W. W. Norton, 1988); and Lynn Margulis and Dorian Sagan, *Microcosmos: Four Billion Years*

of Evolution from Our Microbian Ancestors (New York: Summit Books, 1987). The Gaia hypothesis has been used to reconceptualize other fields in order to address concerns in contemporary life, for example, Ronald S. Laura and Sandra Heaney, *Philosophical Foundations of Health Education* (New York: Routledge, 1990).

5. Estelle R. Jorgensen, "Music and International Relations," in *Culture and International Relations,* ed. Jongsuk Chay (New York: Praeger, 1990), 56–71.

6. An important effort to describe musical learning globally and systematically was undertaken by Alan P. Merriam in *The Anthropology of Music* (Evanston: Northwestern University Press, 1964), ch. 8. I am indebted to his pioneering work in describing music education from an anthropological perspective.

7. Dewey, *Democracy and Education,* 7, 181, distinguished between formal schooling and informal opportunities that are educative, in which information is picked up incidentally by associating with others in the social group or society.

8. Dewey, *Democracy and Education,* chs. 6, 10; John Dewey, *Experience and Education* (1938; repr., New York: Macmillan, 1963), especially chs. 1, 4.

9. Israel Scheffler, *Reason and Teaching* (Indianapolis: Bobbs-Merrill, 1973), 76.

10. Dewey, *Democracy and Education,* 6–9.

11. In "Music and the Liberal Education," in *Philosopher, Teacher, Musician: Perspectives on Music Education,* ed. Estelle R. Jorgensen (Urbana: University of Illinois Press, 1993), 79–93, Peter Kivy is skeptical that the weight of philosophical argument favors the necessary inclusion of music in general education unless music is admitted as part of "tribal identity."

12. William Channing Woodbridge, *A Lecture on Vocal Music as a Branch of Common Education Delivered in the Representatives' Hall, Boston, August 24, 1830, Before the American Institute of Instruction* (Boston: Hilliard, Gray, Little and Wilkins, 1831); Estelle R. Jorgensen, "William Channing Woodbridge's Lecture, 'On Vocal Music as a Branch of Common Education', Revisited," in *Studies in Music* (Nedlands: University of Western Australia, 1985): 1–32.

13. Bruce Wilson, "Documentary History of Music in the Public Schools of the City of Boston, 1830–1850," Ph.D. diss., University of Michigan, 1973.

14. Contrasting recommendations for American public education are found in Mortimer J. Adler, *The Paideia Proposal: An Educational Manifesto* (New York: Macmillan, 1982); *A Nation at Risk: The Imperative for Educational Reform,* Report of the National Commission on Excellence in Education (Washington: United States Department of Education, 1983); and *Growing Up Complete: The Imperative for Music Education,* Report of the National Commission on Music Education (Reston: Music Educators National Conference, 1991).

15. See John Dewey, *Art as Experience* (New York: G. P. Putnam's Sons, 1934), ch. 4, for a discussion of the obstacles to artistic creation.

16. David Aspin, "The Place of Music in the Curriculum: A Justification," *Journal of Aesthetic Education* 16 (1982): 41–55.

17. Scheffler, *Reason and Teaching,* 67–81.

18. For a description of the jazz community see Alan P. Merriam and Raymond W. Mack, "The Jazz Community," *Social Forces* 38, no. 3 (1960): 211-22.

19. John Blacking, *How Musical Is Man?* (1973; repr., London: Faber and Faber, 1976), 98, 44, 45.

20. The distinctions between "knowing that" and "knowing how," procedural and propositional knowledge, advanced by Gilbert Ryle in *The Concept of Mind* (New York: Harper and Row, 1949), especially ch. 2, have raised considerable philosophical interest. I accept the distinction, allowing that there may be various sorts of procedural knowledge and the distinction between "knowing that" and "knowing how" is not as clear-cut or stable as Ryle would have us believe. Propositional uses of know-how are involved in expert judgment, and judgment and intelligence are required to demonstrate know-how. See Israel Scheffler, *Conditions of Knowledge: An Introduction to Epistemology and Education* (Chicago: University of Chicago Press, 1965), 91, 92; and Vernon Howard, *Artistry: The Work of Artists* (Indianapolis: Hackett, 1982), 49, 50, 68, 69.

21. Ryle, *Concept of Mind,* 59.

22. Gilbert Ryle, "Teaching and Training," in *The Concept of Education,* ed. R. S. Peters (London: Routledge and Kegan Paul, ca. 1967), 114.

23. Howard, *Artistry,* 176–85.

24. Clifford K. Madsen and Cornelia Yarbrough, *Competency-based Music Education* (Englewood Cliffs: Prentice-Hall, 1980).

25. Howard, *Artistry,* especially chs. 2, 3.

26. Max Black, "Rules and Routines," in *Concept of Education,* ed. Peters, 92–104; Howard, *Artistry,* 97; Vernon Howard, *Learning by All Means: Lessons from the Arts, a Study in the Philosophy of Education* (New York: Peter Lang, 1992), 73–81.

27. Whereas Ryle, *Concept of Mind,* 42, distinguishes between what Scheffler called "facilities" or "routinizable skills," which do not involve thinking about what one is doing, and critical skills that necessitate conscious thought, consigning facilities to drill, and critical skills to training, Scheffler, *Conditions of Knowledge,* 104, maintains that both facilities and skills are acquired through training.

28. For a description of the apprentice's attitude, see Michael Polanyi, *Personal Knowledge: Toward a Post-Critical Philosophy* (1958; repr., New York: Harper and Row, 1964), 53.

29. William Henry Hill, Arthur F. Hill, and Alfred Ebsworth Hill, *The Violin-makers of the Guarneri Family (1626–1762): Their Life and Work,* introduction by Edward J. Dent (London: Holland Press, 1965).

30. Polanyi, *Personal Knowledge,* 53, notes an art that "cannot be specified in detail" and must be passed on "by example from master to apprentice," making it extremely fragile. It relies upon personal contact to ensure its survival, and if it falls into disuse for a generation the art may be lost. He points, by way of example, to the difficulties modern researchers have in reconstructing the building of violins comparable to those Stradivarius regularly produced.

31. Howard, *Artistry,* ch. 6.

32. Scheffler, *Conditions of Knowledge,* 95, 96.

33. Carl Philipp Emanuel Bach, *Essay on the True Art of Playing Keyboard Instruments,* trans. and ed. William J. Mitchell (New York: W. W. Norton, 1949), 30. As a thorough explication of various elements of keyboard technique and performance practice, and a primarily pedagogical treatise, Bach's *Essay* deserves a closer study by music educators than it has received.

34. Several writers have made this point, notably Iris M. Yob, "The Arts as Ways of Understanding: Reflections on the Ideas of Paul Tillich," David J. Elliott, "Music as Knowledge," John Shepherd, "Music and the Last Intellectuals," and Philip Alperson, "What Should One Expect from a Philosophy of Music Education?" all in *Philosopher, Teacher, Musician,* ed. Jorgensen, 5–20, 21–40, 95–114, 215–42.

35. Dewey, *Democracy and Education,* 275, suggested that "there is no such thing as genuine knowledge and fruitful understanding except as the offspring of *doing.*" Not only is the free participation of the student in the training process essential, but he also noted that without the development of imaginative thought, taste, and intellectual understanding a focus on the physical skills alone may well result in limiting and restricting the usefulness of what is learned (258, 260).

36. Dewey, *Democracy and Education,* 13, 142, saw training as antithetical to a democratic education, residing in "outer action rather than in mental and emotional dispositions of behavior," and contributing to a lack of intellectual involvement on the part of the student in the educational process. The kind of open, mutual, interactive dialogue typical of more egalitarian teacher-student relationships is similar to the human interrelationship depicted in Martin Buber, *I and Thou,* trans. Walter Kaufmann (New York: Charles Scribner's Sons, 1970).

37. Dewey, *Democracy and Education,* 291, 292, noted that these philosophical dualities are antithetical to democratic ideals and ought therefore to be opposed within education. Ryle's principal achievement in *Concept of Mind,* notwithstanding his detractors, is his presentation of a more holistic view of mind that discredited Cartesian dualism or "The Myth of the Ghost in the Machine."

38. Ideas about music arise out of musical practice, and musical practice also emerges out of theoretical ideas about it. See Joscelyn Godwin, *Harmonies of Heaven and Earth: The Spiritual Dimensions of Music* (Rochester, Vt.: Inner Traditions International, 1987). For approaches to music and music education that focus on musical practice and take into account social and contextual issues, see Philip Alperson, ed., *What Is Music? An Introduction to the Philosophy of Music* (1987; repr., University Park: Pennsylvania State University Press, 1994); and David J. Elliott, *Music Matters: A New Philosophy of Music Education* (New York: Oxford University Press, 1995). By overlooking the ideas that give rise to practice in the first place, focusing only on practice may be too narrow a view. Much hinges on how practice is defined and how adequately theory and practice are distinguished.

39. See Howard, *Artistry,* ch. 1, on symptoms of craft and art.

40. This holistic approach is entirely in line with Dewey's understanding of the artistic experience as both doing and undergoing, making and receiving of an art work, and his interest in reconciling intellectual and practical knowledge and skills and understanding.

41. Dewey, *Democracy and Education,* 258.

42. The word *eduction* derives from the infinitive "to educe." I have found no other word that so neatly captures this idea. Percy Scholes encountered a similar problem when he tried to better the term *musical appreciation.* See Percy A. Scholes, *Music, the Child and the Masterpiece: A Comprehensive Handbook of Aims and Methods in All That Is Usually Called 'Musical Appreciation'* (London: Oxford University Press, 1935), 27.

43. Dewey, *Democracy and Education,* especially chs. 4, 5. More recent formulations of this idea may be found, for example, in the emphasis on nurturing in Nel Noddings, *Caring: A Feminine Approach to Ethics and Moral Education* (Berkeley: University of California Press, 1984) and on human potential in Israel Scheffler, *Of Human Potential: An Essay in the Philosophy of Education* (London: Routledge and Kegan Paul, 1985).

44. Dewey, *Democracy and Education,* 49.

45. Ibid., 50.

46. Shinichi Suzuki, *Nurtured by Love: A New Approach to Education,* trans. Waltraud Suzuki (New York: Exposition Press, 1969), 31.

47. Suzuki, *Nurtured by Love,* 55. In this quotation, Suzuki uses the word *educated* specifically with reference to the analogy of the tree to refer to the eduction of "talent." For him, talent is synonymous with ability. It "is not inborn," but "every child acquires ability through experience and repetition" (27).

48. Maria Montessori, *The Absorbent Mind* (New York: Dell, 1967), ch. 3, offers a classification of "periods of growth" that, like other subsequent classifications, emphasizes differences from birth to eighteen years of age. After this, she argues, the person "grows only in age" (20). To treat adulthood as a monolithic entity, however, fails to take account of important physiological, psychological, and sociological developments.

49. For Montessori, "the first two years are the most important in the whole span of human life." *Absorbent Mind,* 4.

50. Montessori agrees that "the central point of education must be the defense of life." Ibid., 10.

51. Noddings, *Caring.*

52. Arnold Berleant, "Musical De-composition," in *What Is Music?* ed. Alperson, 252, 253.

53. Roger Sessions, *The Musical Experience of Composer, Performer, Listener* (New York: Atheneum, 1962), 52, 44, 22.

54. Scheffler, *Reason and Teaching,* 71.

55. Ibid., 76.

56. Alastair Taylor, "Systems Approach to the Political Organization of Space," *Social Science Information,* International Social Science Council 14 (1975): 7–40.

57. For example, Émile Durkheim makes the mistake of assuming that all behavior is socially determined, thereby overlooking other causal aspects in social systems. See Henry Zentner, *A Test for the Validity of Durkheim's Conception of Social Solidarity* (Ann Arbor: University Microfilms Library Services, 1950). Montessori makes a similar mistake of interpreting educational events solely in biological and psychological terms.

58. Gilbert Highet, *The Art of Teaching* (1950; repr., New York: Vintage, 1955), 176–88.

59. Henry Zentner, *Prelude to Administrative Theory* (Calgary: Strayer, 1973), 135–37.

60. Hugh S. Roberton, *Prelude to the Orpheus* (Edinburgh: William Hodge, 1946); Hugh S. Roberton and Kenneth Roberton, sel. and ed., *Orpheus, with his Lute: A Glasgow Orpheus Choir Anthology* (Oxford: Pergamon Press, J. Curwen and Sons, 1963).

61. Zentner, *Prelude to Administrative Theory,* 135, 136. This understanding of socialization stands in contrast to that Merriam espouses in *Anthropology of Music,* 146, following Melville J. Herskovits, *Man and His Music* (New York: Alfred A. Knopf, 1948), in a more restrictive definition of socialization as social learning in early life.

62. Thomas Henry Collinson, *The Diary of an Organist's Apprentice at Durham Cathedral 1871–1875,* ed. with notes by Francis Collinson (Aberdeen: Aberdeen University Press, 1982).

63. Estelle R. Jorgensen, "On the Recruitment Process in Amateur Ensembles," *Canadian University Music Review* no. 6 (1985): 293–318; Estelle R. Jorgensen, "Developmental Phases in Selected British Choirs," *Canadian University Music Review* no. 7 (1986): 188–225.

64. John Shepherd, "Conflict in Patterns of Socialization: The Role of the Classroom Teacher," *Canadian Review of Sociology and Anthropology* 20, no. 1 (1983): 22–43; John Shepherd and Graham Vulliamy, "A Comparative Sociology of School Knowledge," *British Journal of Sociology of Education* 4, no. 1 (1983): 3–18; Graham Vulliamy and John Shepherd, "The Application of a Critical Sociology to Music Education," *British Journal of Music Education* 1 (1984): 247–66.

65. Shepherd, "Conflict in Patterns of Socialization," 22; Harry Haughton, "Music as Social and Cultural Reproduction: A Sociological Analysis of Education Processes in Ontario Schools," *Canadian University Music Review* no. 5 (1984): 38–59; Lucy Green, *Music on Deaf Ears: Musical Meaning, Ideology, Education* (Manchester: Manchester University Press, 1988).

66. B. F. White and E. J. King, The Sacred Harp: *A Collection of Psalm and Hymn Tunes, Odes, and Anthems . . .* (Philadelphia: T. K. and P. G. Collins, for B. F. White and E. J. King, 1844); Buell E. Cobb, Jr., *The Sacred Harp: A Tradition and Its Music,* Brown Thrasher Edition (Athens: University of Georgia Press, 1989).

67. They have acquired what Dewey, *Democracy and Education,* 197, called a "socialized disposition."

68. Ernst Fischer, *The Necessity of Art: A Marxist Approach,* trans. Anna Bostock (Harmondsworth: Penguin Books, 1963); Roger L. Taylor, *Art: An Enemy of the People* (Atlantic Highlands: Humanities Press, 1978).

69. Graham Vulliamy and John Shepherd, "Sociology and Music Education: A Response to Swanwick," *British Journal of Sociology of Education* 5 (1984): 57–76.

70. I concur with Francis Sparshott that musical judgments are made within context-specific situations in which no one particular way of doing music or perspective on it is preeminent, and that of the different ways of relating to music none "are for all purposes better than all the others." See "Aesthetics of Music—Limits and Grounds," in *What Is Music?* ed. Alperson, 86. As in a true conversation, "no one has the last word." Rules by which music may be judged as right, good, or even great are built into these context-specific situations.

71. Dewey, *Democracy and Education,* 2. In a reissue of his *Experience and Nature,* Dewey planned to use the word *culture* in its anthropological sense instead of *experience.* See Jo Ann Boydston, ed., *John Dewey: The Later Works, 1925–1953* (Carbondale: Southern Illinois University Press, 1988), 13:362. I am indebted to Mary Reichling for bringing this citation to my attention.

72. Werner Jaeger, *Paideia: The Ideals of Greek Culture,* trans. Gilbert Highet (New York: Oxford University Press, 1939, 1943, 1944), 1:xxii. Edward Myers, *Education in the Perspective of History* (New York: Harper and Brothers, 1960), 80, points out that the Greek notion of *paideia* implied more than current conceptions of "education" or anthropological ideas of "culture" convey; it included "the humanistic ideal of an ethical-political culture."

73. Dewey, *Democracy and Education,* 121, 123.

74. Henry A. Giroux, "Introduction," in Paulo Freire, *The Politics of Education: Culture, Power, and Liberation* (South Hadley: Bergin and Garvey, 1985), xiii.

75. Freire, *Politics,* 57.

76. Alfred North Whitehead, *The Aims of Education and Other Essays* (New York: Free Press, 1929), 30.

77. For example, in "The Jazz Community," Merriam and Mack describe members of that community as historically poorly educated and isolated from the rest of society; although socialized into the jazz "way of life" they were not active participants in the wider culture as a whole.

78. Jacques Attali, *Noise: The Political Economy of Music,* trans. Brian Massumi (Minneapolis: University of Minnesota Press, 1985).

79. Kivy, "Music and the Liberal Education."

80. K. Peter Etzkorn, "Notes in Defense of Mass Communication Technology," in *The Phonogram in Cultural Communication,* ed. Kurt Blaukopf (New York: Springer-Verlag, 1982), 103, argues that mass communication technology not only individualizes musical experience but also makes it more widely available than would other-

wise be the case. See also his "Contemporary Mediated Music: Challenge to Music Education," *International Journal of Music Education* no. 16 (1990): 3–12.

81. Scholes, *Music, the Child and the Masterpiece.*

82. Maxine Greene, *The Dialectic of Freedom* (New York: Teachers College Press, 1988).

83. Melville J. Herskovits, *Acculturation: The Study of Cultural Contact* (New York: J. J. Augustin, 1938), 14, 15.

84. Lynn Whidden, " 'How Can You Dance to Beethoven?': Native People and Country Music," *Canadian University Music Review* no. 5 (1984): 87–103.

85. *Aristotle's Politics,* trans. Benjamin Jowett, introduction by Max Lerner (New York: Random House, 1943), bk. 7, par. 1332b, notes that we learn some things by habit and others by instruction.

86. Giovani Gentile, *The Reform of Education,* trans. Dino Bigongiari (New York: Harcourt, Brace, 1922), 7–17, 27–31; Robert D. Heslep, *Education in Democracy: Education's Moral Role in the Democratic State* (Ames: Iowa State University Press, 1989), 99.

87. For example, contrary to Arthur J. Todd, *The Primitive Family as an Educational Agency* (New York: G. P. Putnam's Sons, 1913), who saw the preindustrial family's efforts as educational, Heslep, *Education in Democracy,* 99, betrays a culturally chauvinistic attitude when he writes that "we do not describe them as 'educated' unless we believe that their socialization or enculturation is of a kind that embodies their being educated. We may say of a person, 'He is socialized and enculturated, but is he educated?' " This view of education is all the more surprising when Heslep also argues (91) that what counts as education is historically relative. Surely, education must also be spatially relative.

88. The dialectical nature of education can readily be traced, for example, to Aristotle's distinction between subjects that should be studied "merely with a view to leisure spent in intellectual activity, and these are to be valued for their own sake" and "those kinds of knowledge that are useful in business," deemed to be useful, and "exist for the sake of other things" between the "productive" disciplines such as arts and crafts and "practical" disciplines such as statesmanship, prudence, and right actions (*Politics* bk. 8, par. 1338a). See Heslep, *Education in Democracy,* 91. In modern times, it has resurfaced in Freire's educational view of "the dialectical relation between the subjective and objective" and oppressor and oppressed. See Paulo Freire, *Pedagogy of the Oppressed,* trans. Myra Bergman Ramos (New York: Continuum, 1990), 37.

Chapter 2: On Spheres of Musical Validity

1. Sparshott, "Aesthetics of Music," 52, 53.

2. Howard Becker, "Constructive Typology in the Social Sciences," *American Journal of Sociology* 5 (1940): 40–55; Don Martindale, "Sociological Theory and

Ideal Type," in *Symposium on Sociological Theory,* ed. Llewellyn Gross (Evanston: Row, Peterson, 1959); Fritz Machlup, "Homo Oeconomicus and His Class Mates," in *Phenomenology and Social Reality: Essays in Memory of Alfred Schütz,* ed. Maurice Natanson (Hague: Mijhoff, 1970); Philip E. Vernon, "Multivariate Approaches to the Study of Cognitive Styles," in *Multivariate Analysis and Psychological Theory,* ed. Joseph R. Royce (New York: Academic Press, 1973).

3. See the classification of musical styles in Western classical music used in *Music in the Western World: A History in Documents,* selected and annotated by Piero Weiss and Richard Tarushkin (New York: Schirmer Books, 1984) and the classification of musical epochs in Walter Wiora, *The Four Ages of Music,* trans. M. D. Herter Norton (New York: W. W. Norton, 1965).

4. The use of the term *theoretical type* rather than *ideal type* avoids a conflation with normative statements. See Henry Zentner, "The Construction of Types and Standards in Sociology: A Critical Reassessment," *International Journal of Critical Sociology* 3 (1979): 49–59.

5. Theodor Adorno, *Introduction to the Sociology of Music,* trans. E. B. Ashton (New York: Seabury, 1976); Alphons Silbermann, *The Sociology of Music,* trans. Corbet Stewart (London: Routledge and Kegan Paul, 1963); K. Peter Etzkorn, ed., *Music and Society: The Later Writings of Paul Honigsheim* (New York: Wiley, 1973).

6. Etzkorn, ed., *Music and Society,* 130–39.

7. This is notwithstanding opera's portrayal of women or their marginalization in the Western canon. See Catherine Clément, *Opera, or the Undoing of Women,* foreword by Susan McClary, trans. Betsy Wing (Minneapolis: University of Minnesota Press, 1988); and Marcia J. Citron, *Gender and the Musical Canon* (Cambridge: Cambridge University Press, 1993).

8. Alperson, ed., *What Is Music?*

9. Karl F. Schuessler, "Social Background and Musical Taste," *American Sociological Review* 13, no. 3 (1948): 330–35; Paul Randolph Farnsworth, *Musical Taste: Its Measurement and Cultural Nature* (Stanford: Stanford University Press, 1950); John H. Mueller, "The Social Nature of Musical Taste," *Journal of Research in Music Education* 4, no. 2 (Fall 1956): 113–22; Merriam, *Anthropology of Music;* Alan Lomax, *Folk Song Style and Culture* (Washington: American Association for the Advancement of Science, 1968); Mantle Hood, *The Ethnomusicologist* (New York: McGraw-Hill, 1971); Blacking, *How Musical Is Man?;* John Shepherd et al., *Whose Music? A Sociology of Musical Languages* (London: Latimer, 1977); Bruno Nettl, *The Western Impact on World Music: Change, Adaptation and Survival* (New York: Schirmer Books, 1985); Bruno Nettl, *The Study of Ethnomusicology: Twenty-nine Issues and Concepts* (Urbana: University of Illinois Press, 1983); Alperson, *What Is Music?;* Richard Leppert and Susan McClary, eds., *Music and Society: The Politics of Composition, Performance and Reception* (Cambridge: Cambridge University Press, 1987); John Shepherd, *Music as Social Text* (Cambridge: Basil Blackwell, 1991); Susan McClary, *Feminine Endings: Music, Gender, and Sexuality* (Minneapolis: University of

Minnesota Press, 1991); John E. Kaemmer, *Music in Human Life: Anthropological Perspectives on Music* (Austin: University of Texas Press, 1993).

10. On the ways music portends the future see Attali, *Noise;* and Christopher Small, *Society-Music-Education,* 2d rev. ed. (London: John Calder, 1980). In "The Meaning of Music," in *Whose Music?* ed. Sheperd et al., 56, Shepherd posits that "society can only arise and continue to exist by and through the symbols externalised by members of that society"; music constitutes such a symbol system.

11. Charles Ives, "Essays Before a Sonata," in *Three Classics in the Aesthetic of Music* (1920; repr., New York: Dover, 1962), 103–85. Ives was not primarily thinking of content, understood propositionally, but was commenting on the musical devices (be they ideas, themes, or whatever) that not only intrigue the imagination but also carry a spiritual as opposed to a sensuous valence.

12. Georg Simmel, *The Sociology of Georg Simmel,* trans. ed., and introduction by Kurt H. Wolff (Glencoe: Free Press, 1950); Georg Simmel, *The Conflict in Modern Culture and Other Essays,* trans. and introduction by K. Peter Etzkorn (New York: Teachers College Press, 1958); K. Peter Etzkorn, "On the Sphere of Social Validity in African Art: Sociological Reflections on Ethnographic Data," in *The Traditional Artist in African Societies,* ed. Warren L. d'Azevedo (Bloomington: Indiana University Press, 1973); K. Peter Etzkorn, "Social Validity of Art and Social Change," *International Review of Sociology* 10 (1975): 38–48; K. Peter Etzkorn, "Manufacturing Music," *Society* 14 (1976): 12–23.

13. Etzkorn, "On the Sphere of Social Validity in African Art," 344.

14. Immanuel Kant, *The Critique of Judgement,* trans., with analytical indexes by James Creed Meredith (1928; repr., Oxford: Clarendon Press, 1952), par. 40.

15. Kant, *Critique of Judgement,* par. 19.

16. Silbermann, *Sociology of Music,* 90.

17. Fabio Dasilva, Anthony Blasi, and David Dees, *The Sociology of Music* (Notre Dame: University of Notre Dame Press, 1984), 3.

18. Wilfrid Mellers, *Music and Society: England and the European Tradition* (London: Dobson, 1946), 26.

19. Sidney Finkelstein, *Composer and Nation: The Folk Heritage in Music,* 2d ed. (New York: International Publishers, 1989). Finkelstein's observations are consonant with Rose Subotnik's argument in "The Challenge of Contemporary Music," in *What Is Music?* ed. Alperson, 359–96, that contemporary Western classical music has failed to challenge society directly and that its autonomism will eventually lead to its demise.

20. Farnsworth, *Musical Taste,* chs. 1, 2.

21. Robert A. Stebbins, "Music among Friends: The Social Networks of Amateur Musicians," *International Review of Sociology* 12 (1976): 52–73.

22. In "Aesthetics of Music" Sparshott observes (88) that not only is there evident pluralism in musical taste and function, but people also relate in various ways to the

music for which they constitute the public, either as their preferred music, as congruent with or as symbolizing and integrating their life-style.

23. This is as true of the study of world musics that have traditionally focused on formal music making as it is of the emphasis in Western classical music on the music of male composers and performers and literature associated with the music of the church, concert hall, and opera theater, among other formal occasions. In "Music and Male Hegemony," in *Music and Society,* ed. Leppert and McClary, 171, Sheperd suggests that the "vast majority of music consumed in the Western world is concerned with articulating, in a variety of different ways, male hegemonic processes."

24. Henry Zentner, "Sorokin's Analysis of Time and Space," in *Sorokin and Sociology: Essays in Honor of Professor Pitirim Sorokin,* ed. G. C. Hallen and R. Prasad (Moti Katra, India: Satish, 1972).

25. For a modern translation, see Calvin Martin Bower, "Boethius' *The Principles of Music:* An Introduction, Translation, and Commentary," Ph.D. diss., George Peabody College for Teachers, 1967.

26. Max Weber, *The Rational and Social Foundations of Music,* trans. Don Martindale, Johannes Riedel, and Gertrude Neuwirth (Carbondale: Southern Illinois University Press, 1956).

27. Nelson Goodman, *Languages of Art: An Approach to a Theory of Symbols* (Indianapolis: Hackett, 1976), 179.

28. Stephen Jay Gould, *Wonderful Life: The Burgess Shale and the Nature of History* (New York: W. W. Norton, 1989).

29. Attali, *Noise,* 10.

30. Sparshott, "Aesthetics of Music," 76.

31. Penelope Sanger and Neil Sorrell, "Music in Umeda Village, New Guinea," *Ethnomusicology* 19 (1975): 67–85.

32. Steven Feld, *Sound and Sentiment: Birds, Weeping, Poetics, and Song in Kaluli Expression,* 2d ed. (Philadelphia: University of Pennsylvania Press, 1990).

33. Etzkorn, ed., *Music and Society,* 202. Studies of racial and ethnic differences in musical aptitude and ability have been similarly inconclusive. See Rosamund Shuter Dyson and Clive Gabriel, *The Psychology of Musical Ability,* 2d. ed. (London: Methuen, 1981), 210–15.

34. Talcott Parsons and Robert F. Bales, *Family, Socialization and Interaction Process* (New York: Free Press, London: Collier-Macmillan, 1955); Claude Lévi-Strauss, *The Elementary Structures of Kinship,* rev. ed., trans. James Harle Bell and John Richard von Sturmer, ed. Rodney Needham. (Boston: Beacon Press, 1969).

35. Heide Göttner-Abendroth, "Nine Principles of a Matriarchal Aesthetic," in *Feminist Aesthetics,* trans. Harriet Anderson, ed. Gisela Ecker (Boston: Beacon Press, 1985), 81–84.

36. Blacking, *How Musical Is Man?* 37, 44, 49, 51.

37. Daniel M. Neuman, "The Social Organization of a Musical Tradition: Heredi-

tary Specialists in North India," *Ethnomusicology* 21 (1977): 233–45; Daniel M. Neuman, *The Life of Music in North India: The Organization of an Artistic Tradition* (Detroit: Wayne State University Press, 1980), ch. 4.

38. Richard Leppert, "Music, Domestic Life and Cultural Chauvinism: Images of British Subjects at Home in India," in *Music and Society,* ed. Leppert and McClary, 63–104.

39. Chris McCormick, "Maritime Folk Song as Popular Culture: An Applied Study in Discourse and Social Relations," *Canadian University Music Review,* no. 5 (1984): 63–64, 79.

40. Susan Auerbach, "From Singing to Lamenting: Women's Musical Role in a Greek Village," in *Women and Music in Cross-Cultural Perspective,* ed. Ellen Koskoff (Urbana: University of Illinois Press, 1989), 25.

41. Patricia K. Shehan, "Balkan Women as Preservers of Traditional Music and Culture," in *Women and Music,* ed. Koskoff, 45–53.

42. The same is true of families of Western classical musicians such as the Bachs and the Damrosches. See Karl Geiringer in collaboration with Irene Geiringer, *The Bach Family: Seven Generations of Creative Genius* (New York: Oxford University Press, 1954); and George Martin, *The Damrosch Dynasty: America's First Family of Music* (Boston: Houghton Mifflin, 1983).

43. William James, *The Varieties of Religious Experience: A Study in Human Nature* (1902; repr., Harmondsworth: Penguin, 1985); Gerardus Van der Leeuw, *Religion in Essence and Manifestation: A Study in Phenomenology,* trans. J. E. Turner (New York: Macmillan, 1938); Mircea Eliade, *Patterns in Comparative Religion,* trans. Rosemary Sheed (New York: New American Library, 1958); Mircea Eliade, *The Sacred and the Profane: The Nature of Religion,* trans. Willard B. Trask (San Diego: Harcourt Brace Jovanovich, 1959).

44. See Ernst Cassirer, *An Essay on Man: An Introduction to a Philosophy of Human Culture* (New Haven: Yale University Press, 1944), ch. 7.

45. See Iris M. Yob, "The Symbols of Religion: An Analysis of the Ideas of Paul Tillich, Mircea Eliade and Janet Soskice for Religious Education," Ph.D. diss., Harvard University, 1990.

46. See Bennett Reimer, "The Common Dimensions of Aesthetic and Religious Experience," Ph.D. diss., University of Illinois, 1963; Oskar Söhngen, "Music and Theology: A Systematic Approach," in *Sacred Sound: Music and Religious Thought and Practice,* ed. Joyce Irwin, *Journal of the American Academy of Religion Thematic Studies* 50, no. 1 (Chico: Scholars Press, 1983): 1–19; Jaroslav Pelikan, *Bach among the Theologians* (Philadelphia: Fortress Press, 1986); Paul Minear, *Death Set to Music: Masterworks by Bach, Brahms, Penderecki, Bernstein* (Atlanta: John Knox Press, 1987); David Baily Harned, *Theology and the Arts* (Philadelphia: Westminster Press, 1966); Roger Hazelton, *A Theological Approach to Art* (Nashville: Abingdon Press, 1967); Philip H. Phenix, *Education and the Worship of God* (Philadelphia: Westminster Press,

1966), ch. 4; and Frank Burch Brown, *Religious Aesthetics: A Theological Study of Making and Meaning* (Princeton: Princeton University Press, 1989).

47. Goodman, *Languages of Art,* 252, 253.

48. Yob, "Symbols of Religion," 82.

49. Edward Foley, *Music in Ritual: A Pre-Theological Investigation* (Washington: Pastoral Press, 1984); Estelle R. Jorgensen, "Religious Music in Education," *Philosophy of Music Education Review* 1 (Fall 1993): 103–14.

50. Henry Zentner, *Profiles of the Supernatural: Inquiries into the Socio-Psychological Foundations of Religious Behavior* (Calgary: Strayer, 1972).

51. Anne Bagnall Yardley, " 'Ful weel she soong the service dyvyne': The Cloistered Musician in the Middle Ages," in *Women Making Music: The Western Art Tradition, 1150–1950,* ed. Jane Bowers and Judith Tick (Urbana: University of Illinois Press, 1986), 15–38.

52. Stephen Marini, "Rehearsal for Revival: Sacred Singing and the Great Awakening in America," in *Sacred Sound,* ed. Irwin, 71–91.

53. Cynthia Hawkins, "Aspects of the Musical Education of Choristers in Church of England Choir Schools," master's thesis, McGill University, 1985. Examples of choir school histories include Dora H. Robertson, *Sarum Close: A History of the Life and Education of the Cathedral Choristers for Seven Hundred Years* (London: J. Cape, 1938); and Robert J. Henderson, *A History of King's College Choir School Cambridge* (Cambridge: King's College Choir School, 1981).

54. Marion Kilson, *Kpele Lala: Ga Religious Songs and Symbols* (Cambridge: Harvard University Press, 1971).

55. Henry Wilder Foote, *Three Centuries of American Hymnody* (Cambridge: Harvard University Press, 1940). On other aspects of Protestant church music in the United States, see Robert Stevenson, *Protestant Church Music in America* (New York: W. W. Norton, 1966).

56. On the contributions of music educators such as Sarah Glover and musicians such as the Wesleys, see Bernarr Rainbow, *The Land without Music: Musical Education in England 1800–1860 and Its Continental Antecedents* (London: Novello, 1967); Erik Routley, *The Musical Wesleys* (London: Herbert Jenkins, 1968); and Peggy Bennett, "Sarah Glover: A Forgotten Pioneer in Music Education," *Journal of Research in Music Education* 32 (Spring 1984): 49–65.

57. *Aristotle's Politics,* bk. 1, pars. 1252a, 1253a, 1252b; bk. 3, par. 1275b.

58. Ernest Barker, *Church, State and Education* (1930; repr., Ann Arbor: University of Michigan Press, 1957), 190.

59. John Dewey, *The Public and Its Problems,* (Denver: Alan Swallow, ca. 1927), 34–35, described the public as "all those who are affected by the indirect consequences of [social] transactions to such an extent that it is deemed necessary to have those consequences systematically cared for" (15, 16).

60. Dewey, *Public and Its Problems,* 39, 47, 58, 62.

61. Ibid., 66n. Cassirer, *Essays on Man,* 63, agrees that "the state, in its present form, is a late product of the civilizing process."

62. Heslep, *Education in Democracy,* 45, also see 38, 39, 43.

63. Etzkorn, ed., *Music and Society,* 193, 160–200; Finkelstein, *Composer and Nation,* ch. 4.

64. Plato, *The Republic,* trans. Benjamin Jowett (New York: Airmont, 1968), bk. 4, par. 424.

65. Attali, *Noise,* 11, 4.

66. Ibid., 19, 20.

67. Etzkorn, ed., *Music and Society,* 186–99; Finkelstein, *Composer and Nation,* ch. 11; Arnold Perris, "Music as Propaganda: Art at the Command of Doctrine in the People's Republic of China," *Ethnomusicology* 27, no. 1 (1983): 1–28; Richard C. Kraus, *Pianos and Politics in China: Middle-class Ambitions and the Struggle over Western Music* (New York: Oxford University Press, 1989).

68. Attali, *Noise,* 8. See Roger Wallis and Krister Malm, *Big Sounds from Small Peoples: The Music Industry in Small Countries* (New York: Pendragon, 1984), chs. 7, 8, on the exercise of government powers, particularly in ensuring that indigenous cultures are protected and broadcasting is controled.

69. Alan Yorke-Long, *Music at Court: Four Eighteenth Century Studies* (London: Weidenfeld and Nicolson, 1954); Christopher Hogwood, *Music at Court* (London: Victor Gollancz, 1980); Iain Fenlon, *Music and Patronage in Sixteenth-Century Mantua,* vol. I (Cambridge: Cambridge University Press, 1980).

70. Paul Nettl, *National Anthems,* 2d enlarged ed., trans. Alexander Gode (New York: Frederick Ungar, 1952); Percy A. Scholes, *God Save the Queen: The History and Romance of the World's First National Anthem* (London: Oxford University Press, 1954); Conrad L. Donakowski, *A Muse for the Masses: Ritual and Music in an Age of Democratic Revolution 1770–1870* (Chicago: University of Chicago Press, 1977), ch. 2; Roland L. Warren, "The Nazi Use of Music as an Instrument of Social Control," in *The Sounds of Social Change: Studies in Popular Culture,* ed. A. Serge Denisoff and Richard A. Peterson (Chicago: Rand, McNally, 1972), 72–78.

71. Dick Netzer, *The Subsidized Muse: Public Support for the Arts in the United States* (Cambridge: Cambridge University Press, 1978); Mark Blaug, ed., *The Economics of the Arts* (London: Martin Robertson, 1976); Anthony L. Barresi, "The Role of the Federal Government in Support of the Arts and Music Education," *Journal of Research in Music Education* 29 (Winter 1981): 245–56; G. Woodcock, *Strange Bedfellows: The State and the Arts in Canada* (Toronto: Douglas and McIntyre, 1985); Wallis and Malm, *Big Sounds,* 238–39, ch. 7; Hans Werner Henze, *Music and Politics: Collected Writings 1953–81,* trans. Peter Labanyi (London: Faber and Faber, 1982), 201–4.

72. John Janheinz, *Muntu: The New African Culture* (New York: Grove, 1961); Charles Gillett, "The Black Market Roots of Rock," in *Sounds of Social Change,* ed.

Denisoff and Peterson, 274–81; Pearl Williams-Jones, "Afro-American Gospel Music: A Crystallization of the Black Aesthetic," *Ethnomusicology* 19 (1975): 373–85; Finkelstein, *Composer and Nation*, ch. 12; Wilfrid Mellers, *Angels of the Night: Popular Female Singers of Our Time* (New York: Basil Blackwell, 1986).

73. Regula Quereshi, "Ethnomusicological Research among Canadian Communities of Arab and East Indian Origin," *Ethnomusicology* 16 (1972): 381-96; Helen Martens, "The Music of Some Religious Minorities in Canada," *Ethnomusicology* 16 (1972): 360–71.

74. Stanley D. Krebs, "Soviet Music Instruction: Service to the State," *Journal of Research in Music Education* 9, no. 2 (1961): 83–107; Wallis and Malm, *Big Sounds*, 229–31; Frigyes Sándor, ed., *Musical Education in Hungary*, 2d ed. (Budapest: Corvina, 1969); David S. Vassberg, "Villa-Lobos as Pedagogue: Music in the Service of the State," *Journal of Research in Music Education* 23, no. 3 (1975): 163–70.

75. Wallis and Malm, *Big Sounds*, 233–34.

76. Percy A. Scholes, *The Listener's History of Music Complete: A Book for Any Concert-goer, Gramophonist, or Radio Listener . . .* , 6th ed. (London: Oxford University Press, 1943); Percy A. Scholes, *The Listener's Guide to Music, with a Concert-goer's Glossary*, 10th ed. (London: Oxford University Press, 1942); *Everybody's Guide to Broadcast Music* (London: Oxford University Press, and Hodder and Stoughton, 1925); Percy A. Scholes, *The Radio Times Music Handbook . . .* , 4th ed. (London: Oxford University Press, 1950); Carl Orff and Gunild Keetman, *Orff-Schulwerk: Musik für Kinder*, 5 vols. (Mainz: Schott, 1954). In the United States, Joseph E. Maddy, Peter W. Dykema, Edgar B. Gordon, and Catharine E. Strouse had similar involvement with radio music education. See Norma Lee Browning, *Joe Maddy of Interlochen* (Chicago: Henry Regnery, 1963); Henry Dykema Dengler, *Music for All: A Biography of Peter William Dykema* (Baltimore: Gateway Press, 1994); Anthony L. Barresi, "Edgar B. Gordon: A Pioneer in Music Education," *Journal of Research in Music Education* 35 (Winter 1987): 259–74; and Anna E. Brigham, "A History of Music Education by Radio," master's thesis, University of Kansas, 1947. I am indebted to George Heller for these references to American radio music education.

77. Finkelstein, *Nation and Composer*, 166.

78. Ibid., 265–67; Henze, *Music and Politics*, 178–83.

79. Dewey, *Democracy and Education;* Herbert Read, *The Education of Free Men* (London: Free Press, 1944); Herbert Read, *Education Through Art* (London: Faber and Faber, 1958).

80. Lois Choksy et al., *Teaching Music in the Twentieth Century* (Englewood Cliffs: Prentice-Hall, 1986); Michael Mark, *Contemporary Music Education*, 2d ed. (New York: Schirmer, 1986); Polly Carder, ed., *The Eclectic Curriculum in American Music Education: Contributions of Dalcroze, Kodály and Orff*, 2d ed. (Reston: Music Educators National Conference, 1990).

81. Sandor, ed., *Musical Education in Hungary*.

82. Drawing on the work of other sociologists, Robert A. Stebbins, "The Amateurs: Two Sociological Definitions," *Pacific Sociological Review* 20 (1977): 585, takes a similarly symptomatic approach to the sociological definition of professionals.

83. Some societies have been ambivalent about the music profession. Ivo Supičič, *Music in Society: A Guide to the Sociology of Music,* (Stuyvesant: Pendragon Press, ca. 1987), ch. 6, has demonstrated the problems musicians have encountered in supporting themselves entirely by their profession.

84. On this point see Howard S. Becker, "The Professional Jazz Musician and His Audience," in *Sounds of Social Change,* ed. Denisoff and Peterson, 248–60.

85. Supičič, *Music in Society;* Henry Raynor, *A Social History of Music from the Middle Ages to Beethoven* (New York: Taplinger, 1978); Abram Loft, "Musicians Guilds and Unions: A Consideration of the Evolution of Protective Organizations Among Musicians," Ph.D. diss., Columbia University, 1959; Jack B. Kameran and Rosanne Martorella, *Performers and Performances: The Social Organization of Artistic Work* (New York: Praeger, 1983); John Ryan, *The Production of Culture in the Music Industry: The ASCAP-BMI Controversy* (Lanham: University Press of America, 1985).

86. Attali, *Noise,* ch. 3; Raynor, *Social History,* chs. 4, 5.

87. Supičič, *Music in Society,* ch. 6; Percy M. Young, *The Concert Tradition, from the Middle Ages to the Twentieth Century* (1965; repr., New York: Roy Publishers, 1969); William Weber, *Music and the Middle Class: The Social Structure of Concert Life in London, Paris and Vienna* (London: Croom Helm, 1975); Henry Raynor, *The Orchestra: A History* (New York: Charles Scribner's Sons; London: Robert Hale, 1978); Rosanne Martorella, *The Sociology of Opera* (New York: Praeger, 1982). On musical organizations for women, see *Women Making Music,* ed. Bowers and Tick. On the rise of the modern conservatory, see Bernarr Rainbow, *Music in Educational Thought and Practice: A Survey from 800 B.C.* (Aberystwyth, Wales: Boethius Press, 1989), ch. 12.

88. Ian Lawrence, *Composers and the Nature of Music Education* (London: Scolar Press, 1978).

89. Nicholas Wolterstorff, "The Work of Making a Work of Music," in *What Is Music?* ed. Alperson, 108, 113.

90. John H. Mueller, *The American Symphony Orchestra: A Social History of Musical Taste* (Bloomington: Indiana University Press, 1951); James Waddell, *History of the Edinburgh Choral Union* (Edinburgh: T. and A. Constable, 1907); H. Earle Johnson, *Hallelujah, Amen! The Story of the Handel and Haydn Society of Boston* (Boston: Bruce Humphries, 1965); *History of the Handel and Haydn Society of Boston,* 2 vols. (1883–93, 1911–34; repr., New York: Da Capo Press, 1977–79); Robert Elkin, *Royal Philharmonic: The Annals of the Royal Philharmonic Society* (London: Rider, 1946?); M. A. DeWolfe Howe, *The Boston Symphony Orchestra, 1881–1931,* rev. ed. (Boston: Houghton Mifflin, 1931); Michael Broyles, *"Music of the Highest Class": Elitism and Populism in Antebellum Boston* (New Haven: Yale University Press, 1992); Daniel Nalbach, *The King's Theatre, 1704–1867: London's First Italian Opera House* (London: Society for Theatre Research, 1972); Ellenor Handley and Martin Kinna,

Royal Opera House Covent Garden: A History from 1732 (1978; repr., New York: Da Capo Press, 1986); Frederick Corder, *A History of the Royal Academy of Music* (London: F. Corder, 1922); Michael Kennedy, *The History of the Royal Manchester College of Music 1893–1972* (Manchester: Manchester University Press, 1971).

91. Tensions are evident, for example, in the disputes among the English *waits,* German *Stadtpfeifer,* and Italian *pifferi* and their amateur and minstrel counterparts and, more recently, in the relations between amateur and professional musicians in antebellum Boston. See F. H. Shera, *The Amateur in Music* (London: Oxford University Press, 1939); Raynor, *Social History,* chs. 5, 6; and Broyles, *"Music of the Highest Class,"* ch. 6.

92. Stebbins, "The Amateur," 584, 586–87.

93. Ibid., 598, 600–601. For a typology of modern amateurs, see 594-96; also see John Drummond, "The Characteristics of Amateur and Professional," *International Journal of Music Education,* no. 156 (1990): 3–8.

94. On Quantz's apprenticeship see Attali, *Noise,* 16, 17, quoting *Escrits des musiciens,* ed. Jacques-Gabriel Prod'homme (Paris: Mercuire de France, 1912), 351–60. On Mendelssohn's instruction, see R. Larry Todd, *Mendelssohn's Musical Education: A Study and Edition of His Exercises in Composition* (Cambridge: Cambridge University Press, 1983). On piano teacher lineages, see William M. Richards and Richard Sorensen, "Tracing Your Pedegree," *Clavier* (October 1963): 14–18. On the Venetian conservatories, see Denis Arnold, "Orphans and Ladies: The Venetian Conservatories (1680-1790)," *Proceedings of the Royal Musical Association* 89 (1962–63): 31–47; Denis Arnold, "Instruments and Instrumental Teaching in the Early Italian Conservatoires," *Galpin Society Journal* 18 (1965): 72–81; Denis Arnold, "Music at the Mendicanti in the Eighteenth Century," *Music and Letters* 65 (1984): 345–56; and David Larson, "Women and Song in Eighteenth Century Venice: Choral Music at the Four Conservatories for Girls," *Choral Journal* 18 (2) (1977): 15–17. On university music instruction during the Middle Ages and Renaissance, see Nan Cooke Carpenter, *Music in the Medieval and Renaissance Universities* (Norman: University of Oklahoma Press, 1958).

95. Percy A. Scholes, *Puritans and Music in England and New England: A Contribution to the Cultural History of Two Nations* (Oxford: Oxford University Press, 1934), 160, 161; James A. Keene, *A History of Music Education in the United States* (Hanover: University Press of New England, 1982), ch. 2; Jorgensen, "Developmental Phases in Selected Choirs."

96. Margaret Mead, "Community Drama, Bali and America," *American Scholar* 11 (1941–42): 79–88; Merriam and Mack, "The Jazz Community"; William Bruce Cameron, "Sociological Notes on the Jam Session," *Social Forces* 33 (1954): 177–82.

97. For discussion of these welfare considerations, see Mark Blaug, *The Economics of the Arts* (London: Martin Robertson, 1976).

98. Richard A. Peterson and David Berger, "Cycles in Symbol Production: The Case of Popular Music," *American Sociological Review* 40 (1975): 158.

99. Rosanne Martorella, "The Structure of the Market and Musical Style: The Economics of Opera Production and Repertoire: An Exploration," *International Journal of the Aesthetics and Sociology of Music* 6 (1975): 246, 247, 250; Martorella, *Sociology of Opera,* ch. 4.

100. Laurence Kenneth Shore, "Crossroads of Business and Music: A Study of the Music Industry in the United States and Internationally," Ph.D. diss., Stanford University, 1983.

101. Raynor, *Social History of Music,* 39, 40, 42, 45, 83, 88.

102. A. Hyatt King, *Four Hundred Years of Music Printing,* 2d ed. (London: British Library Reference Division, 1968).

103. William Weber, "Mass Culture and the Reshaping of European Musical Taste, 1770–1870," *International Journal of the Aesthetics and Sociology of Music* 8 (1977): 5–22; Weber, *Music and the Middle Class;* and Raynor, *Social History,* 99–104, 139, 140, 154.

104. Clementi's *Introduction to the Art of Playing on the Piana Forte, Six Progressive Piano Forte Sonatinas,* Op. 36, and *Gradus ad Parnassum; or, The Art of Playing on the Piano Forte* illustrate his interest in pedagogy coupled with his publishing and commercial ventures. See Alexander Ringer, "Musical Taste and the Industrial Syndrome," *International Review of Aesthetics and Sociology of Music* 5 (1974): 145, 146; and Martorella, "Structure of the Market and Musical Style."

105. Weber, "Mass Culture," 15.

106. Wiora, *Four Ages of Music,* 161.

107. The distinction between popular and classical music cultures had become apparent by the turn of the nineteenth century and persisted throughout the twentieth century. For Beethoven's insistence that his string quartet in F-minor, Op. 95, should not be performed in public and Mendelssohn's refusal to play his *Songs without Words* (written for female amateur performers) in public, see Ringer, "Musical Taste," 143, 144. For the widespread popularity of rock music in the latter part of the twentieth century, see Simon Frith, *The Sociology of Rock* (London: Constable, 1978), and Simon Frith, *Sound Effects: Youth, Leisure and the Politics of Rock 'n' Roll* (New York: Pantheon Books, 1981). For a discussion of this distinction in the United States, see Lawrence W. Levine, *Highbrow/Lowbrow: The Emergence of Cultural Hierarchy in America* (Cambridge: Harvard University Press, 1988); and Richard Crawford, *The American Musical Landscape* (Berkeley: University of California Press, 1993). According to Wiora, *Four Ages of Music,* 165, the popularization of music runs counter to a genuine folk tradition—a view shared by others, including Zoltán Kodály, *The Selected Writings of Zoltán Kodály,* trans. Lili Halápy and Fred Macnicol (London: Boosey and Hawkes, 1974).

108. Wiora, *Four Ages of Music,* 184–87; Etzkorn, "Notes in Defense of Mass Communication Technology," and G. L. Golovinsky, "On Some Music-Sociological Aspects of the Phonogram: The Record in Soviet Musical Culture," both in *Phonogram in Cultural Communication,* ed. Blankopf, 123–40.

109. Wiora, *Four Ages of Music,* 187, 88; Samuel Lipman, *The House of Music: Art in an Era of Institutions* (Boston: David R. Godine, 1984).

110. Wiora, *Four Ages of Music,* 190, 191; Etzkorn, "Notes in Defense of Mass Communication Technology."

111. See Wallis and Malm, *Big Sounds,* especially ch. 4; Shore, "Crossroads of Business and Music"; Russell Sanjek, *American Popular Music and Its Business: The First Four Hundred Years,* vols. 2 and 3 (Oxford: Oxford University Press, 1988); and Russell Sanjek and David Sanjek, *American Popular Music Business in the Twentieth Century* (New York: Oxford University Press, 1991).

112. Wiora, *Four Ages of Music,* 19, see also pt. iv.; Deanna Campbell Robinson et al., *Music at the Margins: Popular Music and Global Cultural Diversity,* critical response by Simon Frith (Newberry Park: Sage, 1991), 228.

113. Wallis and Malm, *Big Sounds,* 297–311.

114. Nettl, *Western Impact on World Musics,* 20.

115. Peterson and Berger, "Cycles in Symbol Production," 166–67; Frith, *Sound Effects,* ch. 6; R. Serge Denisoff, *Tarnished Gold: The Record Industry Revisited* (New Brunswick: Transaction Books, 1986).

116. Richard A. Peterson, "Market and Moralist Censors of a Black Art Form: Jazz," in *Sounds of Social Change,* ed. Denisoff and Peterson, 236.

117. Wallis and Malm, *Big Sounds,* 117.

118. Peterson, "Market and Moralist Censors," 236. Also see 237, where he notes that the influence of these moralizers is "most clearly evident when the art form is in the process of formation or radical change." Wiora, *Four Ages of Music,* 188–89; Alan Peacock and Ronald Weir, *The Composer in the Market Place* (London: Faber Music, 1975), 31.

119. Denisoff, *Tarnished Gold,* 345, 352, 368–69.

120. Michael Hurd, *Vincent Novello and Company* (London: Granada, 1981).

121. In "Musical Taste," Ringer observes that, historically, "the more trivial types of music appealed to far broader segments of genteel society than the 'serious' works of the acknowledged masters" (148).

Chapter 3: A Dialectical View of Music Education

1. Estelle R. Jorgensen, "Music Education in Broad Perspective," *Quarterly Journal of Music Teaching and Learning* 2, no. 3 (1991): 14–21. Various musicians and educators stand out in history as having taken such a broad view of music education. Percy Grainger, for example, advocated and exemplified a cosmopolitan view of music and music education in his lectures, folk song transcriptions, and compositions, and performances. See John Blacking, *'A Commonsense View of All Music': Reflections on Percy Grainger's Contribution to Ethnomusicology and Music Education* (Cambridge: Cambridge University Press, 1987).

2. Susanne K. Langer, *Philosophy in a New Key; Feeling and Form: A Theory of Art*

Developed from Philosophy in a New Key (London: Routledge and Kegan Paul, 1953), and her *Problems of Art: Ten Philosophical Lectures* (New York: Charles Scribner's Sons, 1957).

3. On Langer's notion of feeling, see Iris M. Yob, "The Form of Feeling," *Philosophy of Music Education Review,* no. 1 (1993): 18–32.

4. Peter Kivy, *Music Alone: Philosophical Reflections on the Purely Musical Experience* (Ithaca: Cornell University Press, 1990).

5. Leonard Meyer, *Emotion and Meaning in Music* (Chicago: University of Chicago Press, 1956).

6. Walter Kaufmann, *The Ragas of North India* (Bloomington: Indiana University Press, 1974).

7. Kodály, *Selected Writings,* 131, posits that just as a person can have only one "mother tongue," so in music it is important to start with one's own folk music.

8. Randel, ed., *New Harvard Dictionary of Music,* 778.

9. Patricia Shehan Campbell grapples with the oral roots of Western classical music and the problems and possibilities of orality in her *Lessons from the World: A Cross-Cultural Guide to Music Teaching and Learning* (New York: Schirmer Books, 1991).

10. Austin Caswell, "Canonicity in Academia: A Music Historian's View," in *Philosopher, Teacher, Musician,* ed. Jorgensen, 129–45.

11. Kodály, *Selected Writings,* 131, 147, 162. Kodály wrote that "by fifty-four well-chosen songs the chief basic phenomena of music could be implanted in the child's soul" (140). He saw that "only art of intrinsic value is suitable for children" (122). In this view, he echoed Friedrich Schiller, who commented on the artist's responsibility as an educator: "Surround them with noble, great and ingenious forms, enclose them all round with the symbols of excellence." *On the Aesthetic Education of Man in a Series of Letters,* trans. with introduction by Reginald Snell (1954; repr., New York: Frederick Ungar, 1965), 55.

12. Kodály, *Selected Writings,* 120.

13. Paulo Freire, *Pedagogy of the Oppressed,* rev. ed., trans. Myra Bergman Ramos (New York: Continuum, 1993); Greene, *Dialectic of Freedom.*

14. Robert A. Choate, ed., *Documentary Report of the Tanglewood Symposium* (Washington: Music Educators National Conference, 1968), 139.

15. Choate, ed., *Documentary Report,* 138.

16. In North America, just as philosophers were calling on music educators to espouse esthetic education as the profession's reason for being, professional leaders were calling on music teachers to revolutionize not only the music profession (and its undergirding esthetic) but also American society.

17. Freire, *Pedagogy of the Oppressed,* 17n. For an analysis of the term *conscientization,* see Freire, *Politics of Education,* ch. 7.

18. Schiller, *On the Aesthetic Education,* letter 9.

19. Scholes, *Music, the Child, and the Masterpiece,* 81; Estelle R. Jorgensen, "Percy Scholes on Music Appreciation," *British Journal of Music Education* 4, no. 2 (1987): 139–56.

20. Dewey, *Experience and Education,* especially ch. 3.

21. On the importance of the present moment, see Whitehead, *Aims of Education,* 14.

22. Philip Phenix, *Realms of Meaning: A Philosophy of the Curriculum for General Education* (New York: McGraw-Hill, 1964); William Pinar, ed., *Curriculum Theorizing: The Reconceptualists* (Berkeley: McCutchan Publishing, 1975); Greene, *Dialectic of Freedom;* and Michael Apple, *Ideology and Curriculum* (New York: Routledge, 1990); William Pinar et al., *Understanding Curriculum: An Introduction to the Study of Historical and Contemporary Curriculum Discourses* (New York: Peter Lang, 1995).

23. See Ralph W. Tyler, *Basic Principles of Curriculum and Instruction* (Chicago: University of Chicago Press, 1949).

24. The role of place as a construct for music curriculum should not be forgotten. See Joe L. Kincheloe and William F. Pinar, eds., *Curriculum as Psychoanalysis: The Significance of Place* (Albany: State University of New York Press, 1991).

25. Erik H. Erickson, *Insight and Responsibility: Lectures on the Ethical Implications of Psychoanalytical Insight* (New York: W. W. Norton, 1964), 153, refers to the "cogwheeling stages of childhood and adulthood" as "truly a system of *generation* and *regeneration."* In his earlier *Childhood and Society,* 2d ed. (New York: W. W. Norton, 1963), ch. 7, Erikson lays out eight stages, from birth to old age.

26. Dewey, *Art as Experience,* 46–47.

27. Alperson, "What Should One Expect"; Hilda Hein, "Performance as an Aesthetic Category," *Journal of Aesthetics and Art Criticism* 28 (Spring 1970): 381–96.

28. Howard, *Artistry,* 14.

29. John Paynter, *Music in the Secondary School Curriculum: Trends and Developments in Class Music Teaching* (Cambridge: Cambridge University Press, 1982); Keith Swanwick, *A Basis for Music Education* (Windsor, Berks.: NFER-Nelson Publishing, 1979); Keith Swanwick, *Music, Mind, and Education* (New York: Routledge, 1988); Keith Swanwick, *Musical Knowledge: Intuition, Analysis, and Music Education* (New York: Routledge, 1994); Keith Swanwick and June Tillman, "The Sequence of Musical Development," *British Journal of Music Education* 3 (1986): 305–39.

30. Schiller, *On the Aesthetic Education of Man,* particularly, letters 14, 15. In the introduction to this edition, Reginald Snell notes Schiller's seeming ambivalence about whether play is an end or a means to an end (15), which he attributes to "Schiller's own extremely rapid transition to dialectical thinking" (16).

31. Judith Vander, *Songprints: The Musical Experience of Five Shoshone Women* (Urbana: University of Illinois Press, 1988).

32. Lois Choksy and David Brummitt, *120 Singing Games and Dances for Elementary Schools* (Englewood Cliffs: Prentice-Hall, 1987).

33. Whitehead, *Aims of Education,* ch. 2; Michael J. Parsons, *How We Understand Art: A Cognitive Developmental Account of Aesthetic Experience* (Cambridge: Cambridge University Press, 1987), ch. 1; Swanwick, *Music, Mind, and Education,* ch. 5.

34. Joseph J. Schwab, *The Practical: A Language for Curriculum* (Washington: National Education Association, 1970); Joseph J. Schwab, "The Practical: Arts of Eclectic," *School Review* 79 (1971): 493–542; Scheffler, *Reason and Teaching,* 181–96.

Index